£2.50

D1792828

Past-into-Present Series

THE ARMY

Peter Lane

Principal Lecturer in History,
Coloma College of Education

B T BATSFORD LTD London & Sydney

First published 1975

© Peter Lane 1975

Computer composed by Eyre & Spottiswoode Ltd
at Grosvenor Press, Portsmouth

Printed by The Anchor Press Ltd, Tiptree, Essex
for the Publishers
B T Batsford Ltd, 4 Fitzhardinge Street, London W1A 0AH
23 Cross Street Brookvale NSW 2100 Australia

ISBN 0 7134 2900 3

For Simon Benedict

Acknowledgments

The author and publishers would like to thank the following for their kind permission to reproduce copyright illustrations: the Radio Times Hulton Picture Library for figs 1, 4, 25, 28, 40, 43, 44, 45, 46, 50; the Trustees of the Victoria & Albert Museum for figs 2, 29, 30, 31, 34, 39; the Mansell Collection for figs 3, 19, 24, 26, 38, 41; Aerofilms for figs 5, 7, 22, 27; the National Army Museum for fig 16; National Monuments Record, Crown Copyright, for fig 17; A F Kersting for fig 21; the Tate Gallery, London, for fig 36; Chichester City Museum for fig 42; Reading Chronicle and Berkshire Mercury for fig 47; the Imperial War Museum for figs 51, 52, 53, 54, 55, 56, 57, 58, 59, 60, 61, 62, 63; Fox Photos for figs 64, 65; Edinburgh University for fig 10; Dorset Military Museum for fig 48. The other pictures appearing in this book are the property of the publishers.

Contents

Acknowledgments 2

List of Illustrations 4

1 The Army as a Mirror of the Nation 5
2 The Army's Predecessors 9
3 The Birth of the Modern Army, 1642-60 18
4 The British Army under Marlborough, 1690-1710 28
5 New Uniforms, and a New Empire 36
6 Wellington's Army, 1800-1815 45
7 The Queen's Army, 1840-80 53
8 The Popular Army, 1880-1914 64
9 The First World War, 1914-18 72
10 The Second World War, 1939-45 82
11 A Post-War Postscript, 1945-70 90

Further Information 94

Index 95

The Illustrations

1	Dead soldiers, 1916	5
2	The Duke of Wellington	6
3	'Valley of Death', Crimea	7
4	Wounded soldiers, 1900	8
5	The Tower of London	10
6	A medieval siege	11
7	Caernarvon Castle	12
8	A belfry	13
9	Medieval knights	15
10	A Tudor army	16
11	General Fairfax	19
12	Types of cannon-ball	20
13	Cavalier gentlemen	22
14	Battle of Naseby, 1645	23
15	A musketeer	24
16	Coronation procession, 1661	25
17	Royal Hospital, Chelsea	26
18	Siege of Namur, 1695	29
19	Battle of Blenheim, 1704	30
20	Battle of Ramillies, 1706	32
21	Blenheim Tapestry	33
22	Blenheim Palace	34
23	A foot soldier, 1742	37
24	A Grenadier, 1780	37
25	Walpole and Captain Jenkins	38
26	Battle of Minden, 1759	40
27	Death of General Wolfe, 1759	41
28	Gordon Riots, 1780	44
29	Battle of Assaye, 1803	46
30	Battle of Talavera, 1809	47
31	Peninsular army, 1811	48
32	The 'diehards', 1812	49
33	Crossing the Pyrénées, 1813	50
34	Chelsea Pensioners	52
35	Landing in Burma, 1825	53
36	'The Remnants of an Army'	54
37	An Indian march, 1858	56
38	The Indian Mutiny, 1857	57
39	'A Wellington Boot'	59
40	Battle of Inkerman, 1854	60
41	Charge of the Light Brigade	61
42	Royal Sussex Regiment Museum	63
43	Boers outside Mafeking	65
44	Boer rush on Spion Kop	66
45	New Zealanders to the rescue, 1900	69
46	The relief of Mafeking, 1900	70
47	Maiwand memorial, Reading	71
48	Volunteers, 1914	72
49	Recruiting poster, 1915	73
50	Gallipoli landing, 1915	74
51	In the trenches	76
52	British Tommy, 1916	77
53	Stretcher bearers at Ypres, 1917	79
54	Tanks in action, 1916	80
55	Soldiers with gas masks	81
56	'Withdrawal from Dunkirk', 1940	83
57	Tanks in North Africa, 1942	84
58	Montgomery in North Africa, 1942	85
59	Desert warfare, 1942	86
60	D Day landing, 1944	87
61	Airborne forces	88
62	'Mopping up', 1944	89
63	Feeding refugees, 1945	91
64	Troops in Belfast, 1971	92
65	New Chelsea barracks, 1962	93

1. The Army as a Mirror of the Nation

The Army, November 1973
Yesterday, 14 November 1973, about 600 million people watched as Princess Anne was wedded to Captain Mark Phillips. Among other things, the world-wide audience saw the British Army putting on a traditional ceremonial display with the Household Cavalry, Life Guards and other regiments adding to the excitement of the colourful day.

Only three days previously, on 11 November, the British people shared with the Army and other armed services the annual National Day of Remembrance, in honour of those who gave their lives in two World Wars. Over 30 million Flanders poppies were sold in Britain in the week leading up to Remembrance Day.

The British Army is not a remote force of which the people have to be afraid; it is one with which they share the pleasure of ceremonial — such as the Changing of the Guard — and the pride and sorrow of Remembrance Day. The Army is very much a part of the nation's life; it is, as will be shown in the following pages, a mirror of the nation's life and development.

1 In the mud of Flanders many thousands of British soldiers died, believing that they were helping to make the world a better place. Every year, on the National Day of Remembrance, we honour the memory of men such as these.

The Army in British History

The modern Army has its origins in the Civil War of 1642-49, which was fought to settle the dispute over whether the King or Parliament was to govern the country. The history of the British Army since then is the history of the British people — winning Empires in India and Canada, defying the power of Napoleon and Russia, winning a wider Empire at the end of the nineteenth century, and fighting two major wars in this present century.

The history of the Army since 1945 is a history of the British people's attempts to maintain their role as one of the world's leading powers, but being forced to abandon that role in area after area so that, by today, the Empire has been converted into a self-governing Commonwealth, and the Mother Country, Britain, has become a partner in the European Economic Community.

The Army and the English Character

Although we write and talk about the British Army, in fact in certain respects it has been, and still is, an English Army. The Irish, Welsh and Scots have played an important but a subordinate part in the Army. And the British Army consequently reflects much of the English character. 'They value themselves too much and think nothing can stand before them' might have been said by the manager of one or other of the football teams which have defeated England since 1970. In fact it was said by a Captain Blackader of the Cameronians after the Battle of Schellenburg in 1704. Equally telling is the remark by a leader of the Mahrattas, an Indian group defeated by the British in 1803: 'They came

2 The great British general Wellington, in a portrait by Thomas Lawrence, 1814. The son of a rich family, Wellington bought his way to promotion, and was a full colonel by the time he was 27.

3 The valley in the Crimea where the Light Brigade went on its obedient way to meaningless death. As one French observer put it: 'It is magnificent, but it is not war.'

here in the morning, looked over the wall, walked over it, killed all the garrison, and retired for breakfast.' The assumption of this 'effortless superiority' has, at least until recently, been an English characteristic. In 1899 an article in *Navy and Army* noted:

> The British soldier is no better than any other, but he has won many battles by virtue of his insufferable conceit. Even when he has been handsomely beaten, this same has prevented him from acknowledging it and retiring from the field, as he ought to have done if he had played the game fairly. But what can you do with men who are so infatuated with conceit that every private soldier says to himself: 'The British Army is the finest in the world, my regiment is the finest in the British Army, and I am the finest soldier in my regiment'? Clearly all argument, mental or physical, is lost on such people.

The Nation and Remembrance Day
In 1918 a Canadian doctor wrote a poem *In Flanders Fields* in which there is this stanza:

> We are dead. Short days ago
> We lived, felt dawn, saw sunset glow,
> Loved and were loved, and now we lie
> In Flanders fields.

In November 1973 some interviewers from BBC television asked people about the poppy and Remembrance Day. Very few had any idea of why it should be called a Flanders Poppy, few knew why we had a Remembrance Day. Flanders is already forgotten. Equally forgotten are the men who fought to defend India from Japanese invasion in the 1940s. On the war memorial at Kohima, in Assam, is an inscription:

> When you go home
> Tell them of us and say
> For their tomorrow
> We gave our today.

The history of the Army is worth studying for its own sake — it is an excellent story of heroes and battles, generals and common soldiers. It is also worth studying because it reflects so closely the history of the British nation. But perhaps the best reason for studying the history of the Army is to remind ourselves of what we owe to the men who fought, and have been largely forgotten.

4 A frontal attack on a rocky hilltop during the Boer War. Captain Foot, who commanded the British troops on this attack, was invited by the Boers to put out a white flag so that the wounded could be helped. Captain Foot's reply was simple: 'No. I will die first.'

2. The Army's Predecessors

Not a Military People?
In 1809 Sir Arthur Wellesley (later the first Duke of Wellington) wrote to the British Minister in Portugal, saying: 'We are not naturally a military people; the whole business of an army upon service is foreign to our habits.'

In fact nothing could be further from the truth. The British have been almost constantly at war in some part of the world, and when not fighting for their own king have offered their services to foreign kings as mercenary soldiers. One of the rights on which Anglo-Saxons insisted was that every freeman should be allowed to carry arms in defence of his land. When King Alfred the Great (849-899) fought a series of wars against the Danes, he tried to organize the freemen into an army (called a fyrd). He divided his subjects into two groups, one to serve with him against the Danes, the other to carry on with their normal work.

The Battle of Hastings
It was this fyrd which Harold led during his brief kingship. In October 1066, he marched into battle with it at Stamford Bridge, and defeated his brother Tostig who had claimed the throne. Then he rushed south to fight against Duke William of Normandy who led a very different kind of army. Harold's men were armed with axes and bows; William's main force consisted of heavy cavalry supported by spear-throwing infantrymen. A priest who also served as a soldier with Duke William has left us an account of the Battle of Hastings. He tells us that the Saxons waited on the top of the hill, standing shoulder to shoulder and shield to shield. At first the Saxons seemed to be on the point of winning:

> ... and hurled back spears, and javelins and weapons of all kinds. You would have thought to see our men overwhelmed by this weight of projectiles ... The English had the advantage of the ground and profited by remaining within their position. Then the foot-soldiers and the Breton knights, panic-stricken, broke in flight before the English, and the whole army of the Duke was in danger of retreat for they believed that their Duke and Lord was killed.

Here we can see the commander's influence and courage which is emphasized in the priest's account when he talks about Duke William:

> Staying their retreat, he took off his helmet, and standing before them bare-headed he cried: 'Look at me well. I am alive and by the grace of God I

shall yet prove victor.' With these words he restored their courage. The English fought to prevent the attackers from penetrating within their ranks, which indeed were so closely massed together that even the dead had not space in which to fall ... The Normans and their allies pretended to retreat. The barbarians thinking victory within their grasp gave rapid pursuit to those whom they thought to be in flight; but the Normans, suddenly wheeling their horses, surrounded them and cut down their pursuers so that no-one was left alive. Twice was this ruse employed and then they attacked those that remained ... At last the English began to weary, and submitted to their punishment. The Normans threw and struck and pierced ...

The Norman Conquest and a Feudal Army

After his coronation at Westminster, King William divided England into 60,000 districts, and gave one or more of these to each of his followers as a reward.

5 William the Conqueror built the White Tower at the Tower of London, hoping thus to overawe the city's inhabitants. Notice the River Thames (*bottom right*) by which the Tower was best approached. Notice also the space around the walls; this is now a lawn, but it used to be a water-filled moat.

Each district was a 'knight's fee' — or the land which a knight would receive in return for promising to provide the king with 40 days' military service a year.

Each knight coming to serve his king would ride his own horse, have his own armour and weapons, and bring with him his own supporters — carrying spears, staves or bows. In addition to this force of upper-class cavalry and lower-class footmen, the king would also recruit others who would be paid out of his own purse. The success of this feudal army depended in the end on the ability of the heavily-armed knights to get among the enemy forces and slay them, kill or capture their leader, and so claim the victory. The infantry had to try to injure or kill the knights and their horses, and to stand up to cavalry charges so that the enemy could not get near their own leader and standard.

This feudal army was not a very strong weapon for an ambitious king. Each knight was only obliged to serve for 40 days — after which he could return home. This was barely enough time for the king to gather an army to march against a rebellious baron inside the country. It was certainly not long enough for a king planning a foreign war. Henry I (1068-1135) realized this, and to compensate for it he brought in a system known as scutage (or shield money). This meant that a knight who did not wish to do his 40 days' service could pay

6 A medieval siege. Some men are trying to scale the walls; others, armed with crossbows *(foreground)* and longbows *(background)*, try to kill the defenders whose heads appear above the battlements. The armoured knights and their attendants wait nearby for the city to surrender.

7 Caernarvon Castle, one of the many castles built throughout Britain after the Norman Conquest. Attack from the sea was difficult, and attackers coming by land could be easily seen and repulsed. There is a legend that it was here that Edward I presented his son to the Welsh chieftains as their Prince.

the king 40 shillings, and the king would then use this money to hire English or foreign soldiers to serve him for as long as the war lasted.

Richard I and the Crusades

You may have seen the statue of King Richard which stands outside the Houses of Parliament in London. He has been described as 'a bad son, a bad brother, a bad king but a gallant and brave soldier'. In 1190 he set sail with an army of 4,000 horsemen and 4,000 footmen to try and recapture the Holy Land of Palestine from the Turks. One of the problems facing any army commander has always been that of discipline — how does a commander make sure that his men behave? One of the men who sailed with King Richard was Richard of Howden. He wrote down the rules of the voyage as issued by the king:

We have had the following regulations drawn up:
Whoever ... shall slay another is himself to be cast into the sea, lashed to the dead man ... If anyone draw a knife for the purpose of striking another ... let him lose his fist. Let a convicted thief be shorn like a prize-fighter; after which let boiling pitch be poured on his head and a feather pillow be shaken over it.

Other commanders would use different methods; all commanders, however, had to march 'with a sword in one hand and a lash in the other'.

Besieging a Castle
You may have seen one or other of the many castles that are dotted around the British countryside. Most of these were built after the Norman Conquest and served as homes and fortresses for kings and barons. During a rebellion or in time of war, the king would have to try to capture the castle of the rebellious baron or of the supporter of a foreign king. The army would make its way towards the castle, often laying waste to the countryside through which it was marching. Vegetables, chickens, pigs, horses would all be seized from the protesting peasants; it is not surprising that the army was unpopular and often feared by the people whom it represented.

Having arrived at the castle, the army would try first to capture it; if this failed, it would then attempt to starve out the castle inhabitants. A siege was a long drawn-out affair in which the advantage lay with the people inside the castle. The attackers used all kinds of weapons to try to get to grips with the besieged. Catapults and slings were built which could throw heavy stones and flaming material into the castle; scaling ladders were put against the castle walls and foot soldiers ordered to climb up; a massive shield — or shed — was also often built. One soldier has described how, 'under its shelter were placed his most skilful crossbow men; ... from this position they worked a crossbow,

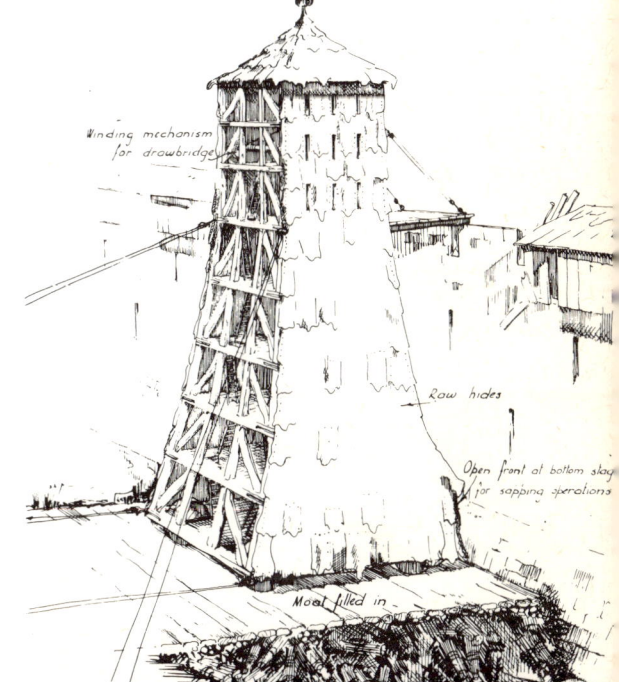

8 A wheeled belfry being used by attackers during a siege. Notice the various ways in which the attackers have tried to overcome the problems presented by the moat and the well-defended walls.

and slew many of the foes by the bolts and quarrels they discharged'.

Then there were various ways of trying to weaken the castle walls; sometimes tunnels were dug under the walls in the hope that this might cause them to collapse; sometimes men were paid to try to tear down the walls. While on Crusade, King Richard paid two gold pieces for each stone taken from the wall under the tower at Acre:

> Then might you see the young men rush against the wall to lug out the stones... The height of the wall was very great and yet, dispelling danger, they extracted many a stone. Turks... strove to cast them down from the walls; and while thus engaged in driving back their enemies, they exposed themselves to darts... One of the Turks did King Richard wound to death, piercing him through the breast with a dart from his crossbow.

If a siege were successful and a castle surrendered, there often followed an orgy of looting and burning, and vengeful killing of men, women and children.

English Bowmen
Some writers suggest that the history of the British Army should begin with an account of the battles of Crécy (1346) or Poitiers (1356), when English longbowmen defeated the French cavalry and bowmen. The English longbow was 6ft (1.8m) long, and could drive an arrow through two thicknesses of mail armour. Edward III encouraged his followers to practise with this Welsh weapon, and the effects of it were first seen at the battle of Crécy, here described by Froissart:

> Then the English archers stepped forward one pace, and let fly their arrows so regularly, and so thick, that it appeared like snow. When the Genoese felt the arrows piercing through their heads, arms and breasts, many of them cast down their crossbows, and cut their strings, and returned discomforted... Then the men-of-arms rushed in among them, and killed a great number of them. And the English still shot their arrows wherever they saw the greatest number. The sharp arrows pierced the men-of-arms, and their horses, and many, both horse and men, fell among the Genoese; and when they were down they could not recover themselves.

There were many sieges of French castles during this long war; one was described by a contemporary:

> Plunder was their ordinary method of provisioning... For purposes of plunder they carried a great many scaling ladders made of separate pieces fitting into each other to take exposed or ill-defended places. A well-defended fortress or walled town they made no attempt to attack. Artillery was scarcely known, and the besieged could always outlast the besiegers, who soon exhausted the supplies of the nearby countryside... The English were noted for violation, burning, extortion, raping, murder and torture,

9 A medieval knight was heavily armoured. Once he had been unseated from his horse it was extremely difficult for him to stand up again and he was vulnerable to attack.

ill-using women in the presence of their husbands and fathers and then demanding ransoms; putting men into irons and drowning those who were not prompt to pay the money demands.

But although men were slain by arrows and swords, many more died as a result of disease. Henry V himself died of dysentery, as did about 23,000 of his men. And when a campaign was over, the former soldiers were discarded, as John Montgomery described in 1560:

10 An English army on the march in Ireland during the last years of the reign of Queen Elizabeth I. Notice the long pikes, the heavy armour and the clumsy muskets.

> When the wars have ended, the soldier's livings and wages also have ended, without any further provisions or other consideration, though they were never so valiant and had won by their worthiness never so much honour to their country and praise to themselves. Many a tall man has lost his life upon the gallows within these dozen years; amongst whom, I have often heard reported, hath been many a good soldier who hath served in many a sharp shower for their princes' honour. Alas! extreme want hath caused them to commit such evil.

This public meanness towards the ex-soldier is a constant feature of the history of the British Army.

Technology

The English may have cheered their soldiers as they marched to board ship for the wars against the French or the Turks. But it was a different matter when the fighting took place on English soil as it did in the fifteenth century, during the Wars of the Roses, when the followers of the House of York fought against the followers of the House of Lancaster. This time it was the English (not the French) countryside that was ravaged, pillaged and devastated. Gradually the aristocratic supporters of each House slew one another until, by 1485, there were only a dozen or so members of the old nobility still left alive. The Wars of the Roses ended with Henry Tudor (Henry VII) acceding to the throne of a war-weary England, whose peasants and farmers, townspeople and merchants were anxious for peace, and opposed to the mercenary professional soldiers who had laid waste to the country.

Henry VII was fortunate in that the recent invention of gunpowder now enabled men to build cannons and other guns which could be used to destroy the walls of castles; the barons and knights who had been able to stand up to the old-fashioned siege were unable to withstand the battering of the besieging army's guns. They soon gave up their warlike habits and transformed their castles into more comfortable homes.

The Tudor Fyrd
The development of artillery also meant that the mercenary soldier was more important than the knight with his armour and horse. Kings now needed men who were experienced in handling the complicated new weapons and guns. Even in the sixteenth century, though, as in the days of Alfred and Harold, every man between 16 and 60 was still liable to be called up to defend his home and country. This 'loyal militia' was often summoned. Sometimes the London militia was called out to parade before the king. With its artillery, drums, fifes and gunners, the procession of 15,000 men took the whole day to parade before Henry VIII in 1540. However splendid they may have seemed, the local militiamen were of little practical use; few of them knew how to use their weapons; few — if any — had any idea of military tactics or discipline; few — if any — had much stomach for a fight. Later trained bands were formed — men who had volunteered for special training. But even these men were of little value, as one colonel admitted:

> As trainings are now used we shall, I am sure, never make one good soldier... After a little careless hurrying over of their postures... the officers make them charge their muskets, and so prepare to give their captain a brave volley of shot at his entrance into his inn; whereafter having solaced themselves for a while, after this brave service very many repair home, and that which is not so well taught them is easily forgotten before the next training.

3. The Birth of the Modern Army, 1642-60

British Soldiers in 1600

We have already seen that Britain at this time did not have a standing, regular army. When the king wished to wage war, he recruited volunteers from among his countrymen and mercenary soldiers from overseas. There were also the trained bands, the descendants of the fyrd, who were supposed to come to the defence of their country if it were threatened with invasion. However, when the bands were called together in 1588 at the time of the Armada, Cornish bands refused to march into Devon, Yorkshire bands mutinied and would not obey their leaders, and almost all the bands were guilty of looting, plunder and pillage wherever they went.

There were, however, other Englishmen who were on their way to becoming professional soldiers. Younger sons of the landed gentry, with little or no hope of achieving fame in their own country, went overseas and joined one of the many armies fighting in Europe. Some enlisted with the famous King of Sweden, Gustavus Adolphus, and fought for the Protestant cause in the wars of religion in Germany. Others went to fight for the Dutch in their struggle against the Spanish. In addition to this officer-class, there were men of the lower orders who joined foreign armies in search of adventure, booty and prize money.

The Civil War

It was these English officers and soldiers who formed the nucleus of the armies which fought each other during the English Civil War. Fairfax, the first Commander-in-Chief of the Parliamentary Army, had fought in Holland with the Dutch. In 1642, when the Civil War began, he commanded an army of 1,000 dragoons, 6,600 cavalry and 14,400 infantry.

Most of the infantry were pressed men — men who had been compelled to join the army. They were divided into musketeers and pikemen — the tallest and strongest men carrying the 16ft (5m) long pikes. There were two musketeers for each pikeman. The musket was a clumsy weapon; even a skilled man would have time to fire only two shots, and then would have to use his musket as a club in a hand-to-hand fight with the enemy. Since the musket had a range of only 20 to 30 yards (approximately 20-25 metres), the musketeers had to walk almost right up to the enemy before firing; then, if they were still alive and unwounded, they had to take part in a charge. It is little wonder that they were known as 'the forlorn hope' — few of them managed to kill or wound any enemy, and once they had fired their two rounds they were almost unarmed, having only their musket to use as a club.

The pikeman, on the other hand, had a better chance of defending himself

11 Sir Thomas Fairfax, the Commander-in-Chief of the Parliamentary Army, 1647.

against a fellow pikeman and, obviously, a much better chance if engaged in a struggle with the poor musketeer. However, it must be remembered that both musketeers and pikemen were raw recruits, dragged unwillingly from field or forge to fight for what they little understood. It was the job of their leaders to turn this 'collection of raw, inexperienced and pressed soldiers' into an army. More than any other man, Oliver Cromwell succeeded in doing this for the Parliamentary side.

Oliver Cromwell

Cromwell was a member of the landed gentry who took up arms against King Charles I for ideological reasons. He and his fellow landowners, with their horses and armour, formed the cavalry – the élite of the armed forces for the next three centuries. The cavalry would wait in a solid mass until the musketeers had fired and the pikemen had engaged in fighting. They would then make a charge – perhaps against a group of enemy infantry who were running away, or against a group of enemy infantry preparing to advance. Cromwell, like others of his class, became an officer when he joined the Parliamentary Army in 1642. In May 1643 a journalist reported: 'As for Colonel Cromwell, he hath two thousand brave men, well disciplined; and no man swears but pays his twelve pence fine; if he be drunk he is set in the stocks or worse.' Cromwell's insistence on discipline marked him off from most other officers, who were in the habit of allowing their men to commit all sorts of crime. Farmers feared the Army, since it used to steal cattle and cut down crops, impose fines and requisition barns and outhouses. Townspeople equally feared these drunken ruffians, who had respect neither for people nor property, as can be seen from a letter written from Coventry on 30 August 1642:

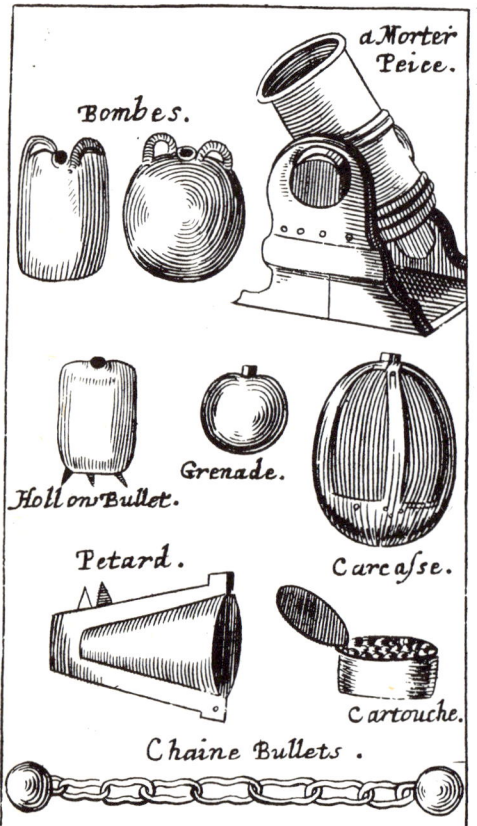

12 Some examples of sixteenth-century cannon and of the projectiles that could be fired.

Our soldiers pillaged a malignant fellow's house in the city, and the Lord Brooke immediately proclaimed that whosoever should for the future offend in that kind should have martial law ... Friday several of our soldiers, both horse and foot, sallied out of the city unto the Lord Dunsmore's park, and brought from thence great store of venison, which is as good as ever I tasted. And ever since they make this their daily practice, so that venison is almost as common with us as beef with you.

Cromwell's insistence on discipline was one of the reasons why he was made Commander-in-Chief of the Parliamentary Army in 1650. Discipline was important because it was only well-disciplined troops that could behave properly on a battlefield. Undisciplined men would throw down their arms and run — making easy prey for cavalry; nor would undisciplined troops have the nerve to carry out an order to march to face an enemy rank of musketeers and pikemen.

Cromwell was responsible for two other major changes. He organized the artillery which few officers had previously bothered to use. His army had 56 guns, some with a calibre of 6 or 7 inches (15-17 cm), and some mortars that could throw 12-inch (30-cm) bombs. The artillery was stationed behind the infantry and, when commanded, fired at the enemy's ranks. This pounding tore holes in the ranks of massed infantry — and caused panic among undisciplined troops. Disciplined troops, on the other hand, would simply fill up the gaps that had been created.

Cromwell's other reform was to order all soldiers to wear the red coat which his own troops had worn from the start of the war. In this way the British Army adopted a uniform which was not fully abolished until 1914. This was not the only way in which Cromwell tried to help his men; he also saw to it that each man was paid (as much as he would have earned as ploughman or carter), and was given a daily ration of bread and cheese — the staple diet of ordinary people at the time. Each man also carried a portion of a tent so that a troop would be able to make camp for the night when ordered.

The Regiment
Meanwhile, King Charles I also had an army. In 1642 he had given a number of his aristocratic supporters the task of raising regiments. He gave to each a sum of money — to pay for uniforms, weapons, food and so on. Each regimental commander would appoint a recruiting officer to get enough volunteers, or else compel men to join the regiment. The regiment took the name of its commander, so we have Gibson's Regiment (now the Gloucestershire Regiment), Meredith's Regiment (now the Royal Hampshire Regiment), and so on.

After the Civil War
Cromwell and the Parliamentarians defeated Charles I, who was executed in 1649, after which Cromwell ruled the country as Lord Protector. We are not concerned in this book with the history of the Civil War, nor with the reasons

13 A window in the church at Farndon in Cheshire, showing some of the 'Cheshire Gentlemen' who served under Charles I during the Civil War. Notice the various weapons that they would have used during the war.

why the British people welcomed Charles II back as King in 1660. This was after a Cromwellian — General Monk — had led an army to London from Berwick in Scotland in order to force Parliament to issue an invitation to Charles (then in exile in Holland). As a reward for this, Charles II allowed Monk's regiment to be called the Coldstream Guards, named after the stream they had crossed when leaving Berwick. In 1675, the King announced that the Coldstream Guards were to be regarded as the second regiment in the British Army.

In 1660 a number of regiments had been formed — supposedly to defend the restored King from the possibilities of assassination by some fanatical Parliamentarians. Colonel Russell was allowed to raise a regiment of Guards, the Earl of Oxford a regiment of Cavalry (the First Life Guards) and Lord Gerard a troop of Horse Guards. In addition, the Duke of York's regiment was recalled from Holland to become the Second Life Guards.

By 1715 there were 21 regiments formed, and the British Army had been born. Each regiment took the name of its commanding officer — who regarded the regiment as his own property, so that we read in a diary: '12 June 1708, Colonel Southwell has sold his regiment for £5,000 to Colonel Hansom of the Guards.'

The Grenadiers

In 1678 the King assigned a troop of Grenadiers to each regiment. These were men specially trained to attack enemy fortifications; armed with axes and carrying scaling ladders, they were supposed to force entry into a besieged town or camp and so make way for the infantry and cavalry. In 1740 a famous song was written about these men:

> Some talk of Alexander and some of Hercules
> Of Hector and Lysander, and such great names as these;
> But of all the world's great heroes, there's none that can compare,
> With a tow, row, row, row, row, row, to the British Grenadiers.
> Where'er we are commanded to storm the palisades,
> Our leaders march with fuses and we with hand grenades,
> We throw them from the glacis, about the enemies' ears,
> Sing tow, row, row, row, row, row — the British Grenadiers.

Recruiting

Each regiment was responsible for its own recruiting. The colonel appointed a recruiting officer and, along with a drummer or two, a sergeant and a few

14 The Battle of Naseby, 14 June 1645, which ended in the defeat of Charles I. Notice the regular formation of the opposing forces; they give the impression of being 'pieces' on a chessboard, waiting to be 'moved' as the commander saw fit. There was no room in these armies for individual initiative on the part of the ordinary soldier.

15 A musketeer. In his right hand is the grooved stick which he shoves into the ground, and on which he balances his clumsy and heavy musket.

infantrymen, the recruiter would tour the countryside offering a signing-on gift of a few pounds and an adventurous life with perhaps great rewards to come. In *The Recruiting Officer* (1706), the playwright George Farquhar portrays a recruiter:

> If any gentlemen, soldiers or others have a mind to serve Her Majesty, and pull down the French king; if any prentices have severe masters, any children have undutiful parents; if any servants have too little wages, or any husband too much wife, let them repair to the noble Sergeant Kite, at the sign of the Raven in this good town of Shrewsbury, and they shall receive present relief and entertainment. Gentlemen, I don't beat my drum here to ensnare or inveigle any man; for you must know, gentlemen, that I am a man of honour! Besides, I don't beat up for common soldiers: No, I list only grenadiers — Grenadiers, gentlemen!

When a recruit joined his regiment he joined a family of men who had a common tradition. They had their stories of members of the regiment who had shown outstanding bravery, and were taught by their officers that it was their duty to uphold the regimental honour. In *The Soldier's Pocket Book* a leading general wrote: 'The soldier is a peculiar being that can alone be brought to the highest efficiency by inducing him to believe that he belongs to a regiment that is infinitely superior to the others round him.'

The Unpopular Army

The soldier who joined did so for life, and from 1660 onwards received 2½p a day in pay (and there was no increase in pay until the 1880s). But the soldier saw little, if any, of this money; 2p was taken away by the company captain to pay for food and clothing, and the rest of it was kept by the regiment to pay for regimental expenses. The company captain paid 1½p to the innkeeper where the man was billeted and used the remainder to pay for laundry and so on.

16 Troops guarding King Charles II through London on his way to his coronation, 23 April 1661.

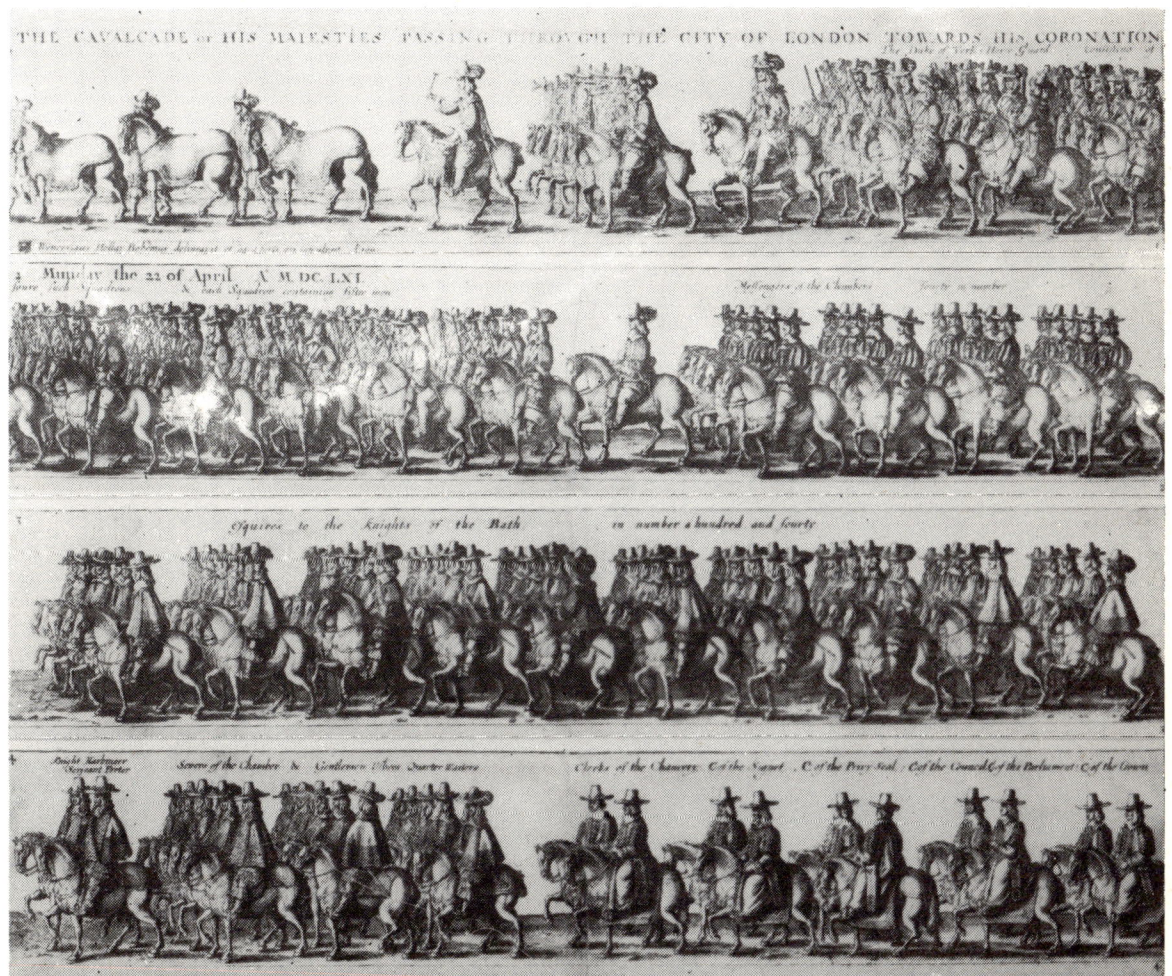

It is not surprising that few people wanted to join the Army, nor that when a man was 'gone for soldier' it was regarded as a disgrace to his family. The government could have recruited all the men it needed if it had offered a fair system of payment and had tried to provide the men with decent living accommodation. But not until the 1780s were there any barracks, so that until then men were billeted in inns and coaching houses, or in private homes. One of the reasons why King James II became unpopular in the 1680s was because he tried to maintain a large standing army in a camp on Hounslow Heath — with which he hoped to frighten the merchants and bankers of London, who were opposing his attempt to restore Catholicism to the country. In 1688 part of the Army, led by John Churchill, transferred its loyalty to James's sister Mary and her husband William, who were invited to become joint rulers. This led to a short struggle between the forces of James II and those who supported William and Mary.

Shortly afterwards, in 1702, the *London Spy* carried an account of the common soldier:

17 The Royal Hospital, Chelsea, showing the river front. The Hospital was designed by Sir Christopher Wren. After 1777, it was used as a refuge for old and disabled soldiers.

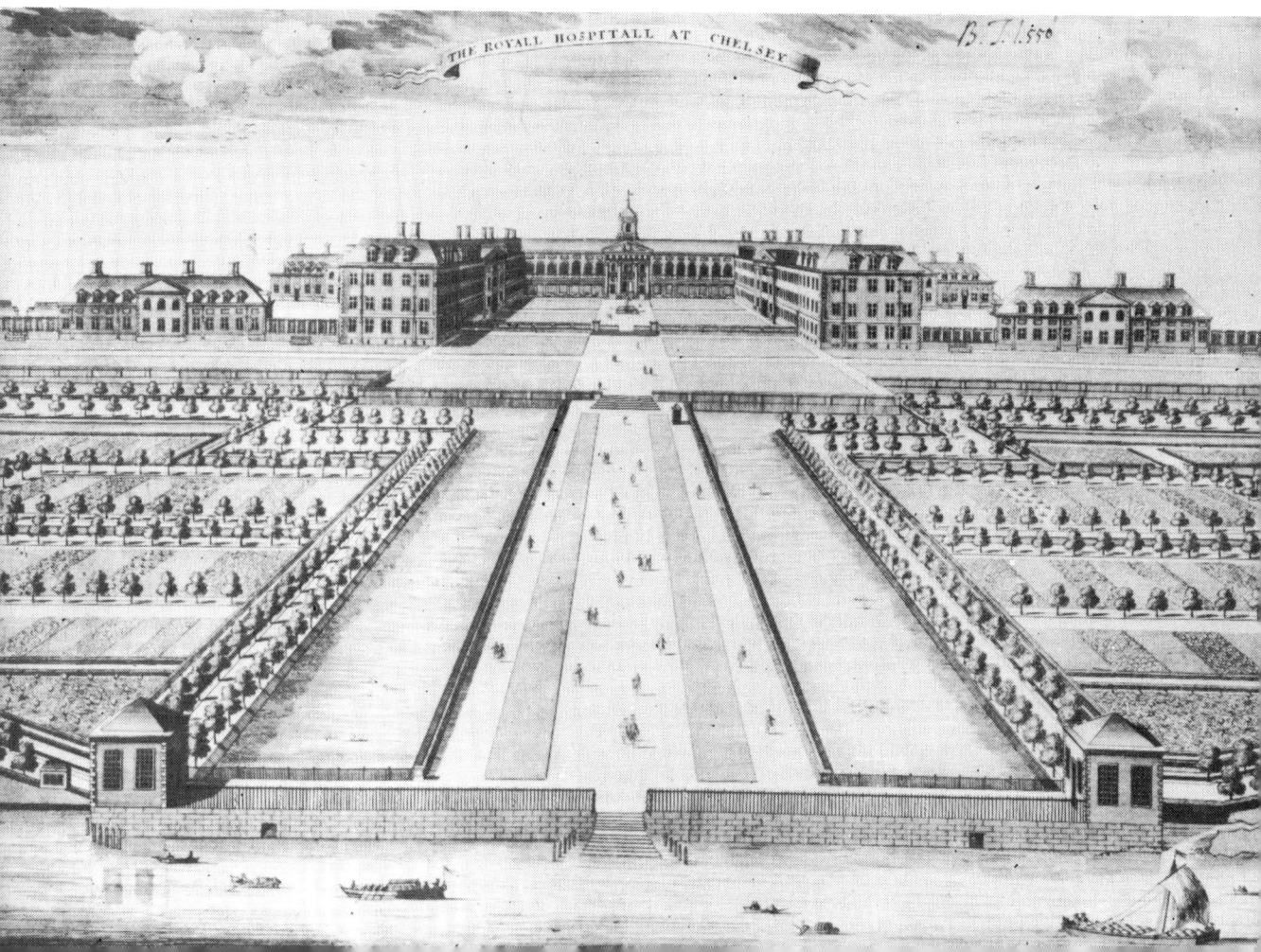

A foot soldier is commonly a man who is coaxed from a handicraft trade to bear arms for his King and Country, whereby he has the hopes of nothing but to live starvingly. His lodging is as near Heaven as his quarters can raise him; and his soul generally is as near Hell as a profligate life can sink him . . . He's one that loves fighting no more than other men; tho' perhaps a dozen of drink and an affront will make him draw his sword . . . The best he can expect to make is to die in the bed of honour; and the greatest living marks of his bravery, to recommend him at once to the world's praise and pity, are crippled limbs.

But the private soldier might argue that he was doing his duty by his country — fighting in Ireland, Ceylon, India, Canada, various countries in Europe — and for what? One, writing from Flanders to his uncle, said:

For I must deal plainly with you I am very weary of a soldier, our pay is very small, we have much to do to live. I have not had one letter from my brother Edmund since I come in to Flanders, he hath been very unkind to me . . .

And if the soldier were injured and forced to leave the Army, what happened to him? One petition from Essex magistrates tells us what happened in 1709:

During the war with France many poor, sick, lame, maimed and disabled soldiers have been weekly brought over in the packet-boats from Holland to Harwich, which have been relieved and conveyed with horses, carts and waggons from there to Bow, in the County of Middlesex, being about three score miles [60 miles, or 96 km]. The charges of relieving and conveying these passengers hath been annually so very great that the monies yearly raised in the said county, pursuant to the said statutes, have not been sufficient to bear the charge . . . We petitioners humbly pray that such future provision may be made for relief and conveying such poor soldier passengers as should be necessary for their subsistence.

One effect of this was that men were even less willing to join the Army. So in 1702 the government passed the Mutiny Act by which any committed criminal who joined the Army received a free pardon for his crime; in 1703 poor law authorities were paid a pound for every pauper that they could force into the Army. Was this a compliment or an insult to the Army? Is it surprising that men recruited in this way were an undisciplined rabble who needed the harsh punishments such as those described in *Tristram Shandy,* when a grenadier who had stolen a few pounds was whipped to the point where he begged to be put out of his agony?

4. The British Army under Marlborough, 1690-1710

British History and the Army

Between 1660 when Charles II was restored to the throne and 1760 when George III came to the throne, Britain grew into the most powerful imperial country in the world — having defeated France in Canada, India and the West Indies. And it was largely Britain's Army and Navy which won this Empire.

Midway through that period, between 1690 and 1740, Britain's Army led by John Churchill, later the Duke of Marlborough, played a major role in defeating the ambitious King Louis XIV of France who was trying to dominate Europe by conquering the Low Countries (Belgium and Holland), defeating the Protestant rulers of Germany, and joining Spain and France together under one king.

The Army, 1672-76

We have to remember that the population of Britain in 1689 was only about five million. The Army with about 50 regiments consisted of only about 30,000 men. Manpower was a very precious commodity and Army commanders were reluctant to waste it in set battles. As you can see from the next extract, a year or more might go by without any fighting taking place.

This is an account of the progress made by the Duke of York's Army which, in 1672, was engaged in war against Holland.

> This siege was carried on with such application that the besiegers were ready in a few days for a storm. We expected the Imperial General, Count Souches, to join us. But he sent some very frivolous excuses of the inconveniency of the ground for a battle and marched off quite another way... The Prince of Orange ordered ten thousand men to march to the siege of Grave.
>
> On his arrival things began to find new motion and the besieged desired to capitulate. Upon which hostages were exchanged and articles agreed upon next morning... The garrison marched out with drums beating and colours flying two days after, and were conducted to Charleroy.
>
> The year 1675 yielded very little remarkable in our Army. Limburg was besieged by the French, the Prince of Orange decamped in order to raise the siege. But while we were on a full march word was brought that the place had surrendered the day before, upon which advice the Prince after a short halt made his little army march back to Brabant. Nothing of moment after this occurred all that campaign. In the year 1676 the Prince of Orange resolved on the important siege of Maestricht... it was accordingly invested about the middle of June.

Notice how little was done in 1675, while it was June before anything noteworthy happened in 1676. Notice too the almost courteous way in which the siege ended. Army commanders tried to insist that a defeated enemy should be treated honourably, although it was almost impossible for officers to prevent their men from looting and plundering the town after it had submitted. Kit Welch was wife of one of Marlborough's soldiers. After the siege of Tournai she wrote:

> During this siege, or indeed any other, I never lost an opportunity for marauding. To this end I was furnished with a grappling iron and a sword, for I must acquaint my reader, that on the approach of an army, the boors throw their plate, copper, etc, into wells... With my grapple I searched all the wells I met with, and got good booty, sometimes kitchen utensils, brass pails, pewter dishes etc, sometimes a silver spoon.

Marlborough's Marches

Marlborough was unlike other commanders in that he sought out the enemy's forces and engaged in huge battles. In order to succeed in this he had to force

18 The siege of Namur, 1695. Namur is built on the River Meuse (*right-hand corner*) which acted as a moat for the town. The town was also defended by a series of outer and inner walls which made attack very difficult. The attackers (*left foreground*) were rarely able to capture a well-defended town.

19 'A Faithful Drawing of the Battle of Blenheim', 1704. Notice the position of the Commander (*left-hand foreground*) and the formation of his forces below. Once again there is the impression of 'pieces' waiting to be 'moved'.

his men to march about 12 miles (20 km) a day for six days at a stretch. Captain Robert Parker was one of Marlborough's officers. He wrote:

> We frequently marched three, sometimes four days successively and halted a day. We generally began our march about three in the morning and reached our ground about nine... Commissaries were appointed to furnish us with all manner of necessaries for man and horse. These were brought to the ground before we arrived, and the soldiers had nothing to do but to pitch their tents, boil their kettles and lie down to rest. Surely was never such a march carried out with more order and regularity, and with less fatigue to both man and horse.

Parker was writing about the Army's march from the Netherlands to the River Danube. On the way the Army laid waste to Bavaria — where the ruler was friendly to France. Kit Welch wrote:

> We spared nothing, killing, burning, or otherwise destroying whatever we could not carry off. The bells of the churches we broke to pieces, that we might bring them away with us. I filled two bed-ticks, after having thrown out the feathers, with bell-metal, men's and women's clothes, some velvets and about a hundred Dutch caps, which I had plundered from a shop; all of which I sold by the lump to a Jew, who followed the army to purchase our pillage for four pistoles.

Blenheim

On 13 August 1704 Marlborough's Army reached Blenheim where the French were encamped. Captain Parker told us what happened when the French found that Marlborough had caught up with them:

> They sent their tents, baggage and everything of value to the town of Hochstet, which was about half an English mile in their rear. Then they drew up in order of battle . . . The Danube on their right, close to which was the village of Blenheim, on their left a large thick wood with a rivulet in their front which made the ground in most places about it swampy and marshy. The Elector and Marsin drew up their part of the army close to the morass . . . Tallard posted in the village of Blenheim 28 battalions and 12 squadrons of dragoons. There were two mills on the rivulet a little above Blenheim in which he posted two battalions . . . He had 70 squadrons on whom was his great dependence. These and his 10 battalions he drew up on the height of the plain, almost half an English mile from the morass . . . Now these with the troops in Blenheim and in the mills were to march out as soon as they saw the Duke pass the morass and fall on his rear. By this means Tallard was sure of having him in a trap between two fires.

You can make a rough sketch map of the way in which the French Army was arranged by its commander who, like all commanders, regarded his squadrons and companies as so many chess pieces which he used in his struggle with the enemy. Marlborough was equally the director of chess pieces. Parker goes on to tell what happened when the Duke gave the order for the infantry to attack:

> Brigadier Rowe at the head of the British Guards and two British Brigades attacked those in Blenheim . . . Brigadier Rowe had proceeded within thirty paces of the pales about Blenheim before the enemy gave their first fire, by which a great many brave officers and soldiers fell. But this did not discourage their gallant commander from marching directly up to the very pales, on which he struck his sword before he suffered a man to fire.

Notice the way in which the commander ignored the deaths of many men while he marched towards the enemy. The men also had been taught to ignore this sort of slaughter — more of which they would have seen while they were standing in their ranks being bombarded by the enemy cannon. One of the reasons for the harsh discipline and seemingly senseless drill was to ensure that men were so well-trained that nothing prevented them from obeying their officers' commands.

And so the first stages of a battle proceeded — artillery duels and infantry charges. Parker, writing about this, tells us:

> It would be impossible to describe in words strong enough the details of the carnage that took place during this first attack, which lasted a good hour or more. We were all fighting hand to hand, hurling them back as they clutched at the parapet; men were slaying or tearing at the muzzles of guns and the bayonets which pierced their entrails; crushing under their feet their own wounded comrades, and even gouging out their opponents' eyes with their nails.

But the battle was not to be won by artillery or infantry, for as Parker wrote:

> The Duke, now finding the enemy very backward in renewing the battle, and as it seemed in rather a tottering condition, sent orders to all his cavalry to advance gently until they came pretty near to them, and then to ride on a full trot up to them... It decided the fate of the day. The French fire was quite extinguished; they made not the least resistance, but gave way and broke at once. Our squadrons drove through the very centre of them, which put them to an entire rout.

Marlborough's Losses
On the evening of the battle, Marlborough wrote to his wife Sarah:

> August 13th 1704
> I have not time to say more, but to beg you will give my duty to the Queen, and let her know that Her Army has had a Glorious Victory!

20 The pursuit of the French after the Battle of Ramillies, 1706.

21 The huge Blenheim Tapestry which hangs in Blenheim Palace (*see picture* 22).

However, other people took a different view of a battle in which the allied armies led by Marlborough lost 12,000 men killed or seriously wounded — nearly a quarter of their force. This was quite unlike the experience of the more casual warfare of the past. The poet Robert Southey (1774-1843) wrote:

> They say it was a shocking sight
> After the field was won,
> For many thousand bodies here
> Lay rotting in the sun;
> But things like that, you know, must be
> After a famous victory.

And this was not the end; there were equally bloody battles at Ramillies (1706), Oudenarde (1708), and Malplaquet (1709). The British government was forced to pass a number of Army Recruiting Acts to try to fill the gaps left by the losses suffered under Marlborough. In 1711 Marlborough was dismissed by the government and went into exile in Holland, where he lived until 1714.

Marlborough's Genius

Marlborough's first task had been to inspire his men with confidence in his leadership. A Prussian officer who was fighting at Oudenarde wrote: 'My lord Duke shone in the battle, giving his orders with the greatest sangfroid, exposing his person to danger like the commonest soldier.'

The modern commander is unable to take an active part in the battle; but Marlborough could sit on horseback on the top of a hill and direct affairs from there — either sending messengers with instructions to his officers, or himself galloping to issue orders or take command of a sector of the battle. Parker was at Ramillies. He wrote: 'The Duke was in all places where his presence was requisite... his presence animated them [the men] to that degree that they pressed home upon the enemy and made them shrink and give back.'

Marlborough's second task — and that of any modern commander — was to out-think the enemy. We have already seen one account of the enemy's arrangements at Blenheim. Here is an extract from another account of that battle, given by Colonel Park. Compare this with Parker's account and notice in what respect the Duke has out-thought the enemy:

> The Duke ordered a little rivulet and morass in front of the enemy to be sounded and where it was found to be impassable, he caused bridges to be made in the face of the enemy ... Prince Eugene being hard pressed by the Bavarians began to give way: which his Grace perceiving, went in person thither, and ordered the *corps de réserve* to advance, and saw them himself pass over the rivulet, and there formed them, which put a stop to the enemy's advancing any further ... The Duke of Marlborough had been 16 hours on horseback and was in pursuit of the enemy when this express came away.

Conditions for the Troops

And what sort of people were the Duke's English troops? They were dressed in long redcoats and breeches, and wore cocked hats on their head. Most had been recruited from villages and towns by individuals like the Recruiting Officer in George Farquhar's play (see page 24). Campaigns were conducted during the summer only — so that recruiting was done in the winter time. Farquhar's play contains a verse about the new recruits:

> Over the hills and over the main,
> To Flanders, Portugal and Spain,
> The Queen commands, and we'll obey
> Over the hills and far away.

Mathew Bishop was a landowner, and an officer in Webb's regiment (the 8th Foot). He wrote: 'We got two three bushels of beans, and a bushel of wheat at a time; so some days we had boiled beans, and sometimes when we mounted

22 A grateful Queen and Parliament rewarded Marlborough with, among other things, Blenheim Palace. Marlborough's soldiers were less fortunate.

the trenches, we made ourselves dumplings, which we thought extremely good living.'

On his long marches Marlborough was careful to ensure that the men's food was prepared for them; the men were grateful for this efficiency and nicknamed him Corporal John. But not even Marlborough could organize an efficient medical service; men who dropped out on a march were left behind, or dragged by their comrades to the next village where they were left. After the siege of the town of Tournai, Kit Welch wrote:

> When Captain Brown was mounting the trench, he had his leg so miserably shattered by a musket-shot that the surgeon was obliged to cut it off. His servants and nurses not having the courage to hold the candle, I performed that office and was very intent on the operation, which no way shocked me, as it was absolutely necessary.

The Army in Peacetime
The historian Trevelyan wrote: 'Marlborough's victories helped to make England proud of her soldiers, yet the treatment of Marlborough himself in the last years of Anne shows how little, even then, the country cared for a Redcoat or was dazzled by the glory of war.'

The country cared even less for Marlborough's Army once the wars were over, and the Peace of Utrecht signed in 1713. In that year there were 200,000 men in the Army; by 1720 there were only 18,000 — the remainder having been dismissed with no reward other than what they had managed to pick up for themselves.

A few of the injured were lucky and got a place at the Chelsea Hospital; the majority of those who were injured became beggars. Those who still remained in the Army were billeted in alehouses or on private citizens. People who had once cheered the Army on its way to France and at the news of the great victories now agreed with the sentiments of the petition sent to Parliament by the innkeepers of Winchester:

> Twenty-six public houses in the said city and suburbs have lately given account of having a great number of soldiers quartered in the said city. This has reduced the number of public houses to four inns and thirty-two small public houses. The Petitioners, if not speedily redressed, must be obliged to give up their houses, or be totally ruined... the Petitioners implore the House to take their hard case under consideration and give them such relief in the premises as the House shall think meet.

As Kipling wrote on a later occasion:

> For it's Tommy this, an' Tommy that, and 'Chuck him out, the brute!'
> But it's 'Saviour of 'is country' when the guns begin to shoot.
> Then it's Tommy this, an' Tommy that, an' 'Tommy, 'ow's your soul?'
> But it's 'Thin red line of 'eroes' when the drums begin to roll.

5. New Uniforms, and a New Empire

New Uniforms

In 1727 George II came to the throne. He had fought at Oudenarde under Marlborough and took an active interest in military matters. Unfortunately for the men most of his interest showed itself in his insistence on new uniforms. The loose breeches which men had worn were replaced by tight, white thigh gaiters (as a concession to common sense the colour was changed in 1767 to black). Even worse was the decision that men's hair had to be worn in a pigtail and whitened with flour paste.

The pigtail or 'queue' took twelve months to grow to the prescribed length and thickness — checked regularly by a sergeant when men paraded. Some commanders insisted on the queue being pulled 'hard and tight' so that men on guard would be unable to sleep. Some did, however, and as one quartermaster wrote: 'It was no uncommon thing when on the guard bench and asleep, to have rats scrambling about our heads, eating the stuff with which our hair was covered.'

A boy, John Shipp, joined the Army in 1795 and has left us a very accurate account of the operation of having a pigtail tied for the first time:

> A large piece of candle-grease was applied, first to the sides of my head, then to the hind long hair. After this, the same kind of operation was performed with nasty stinking soap... When this operation was over... a large pad, or bag, was filled with sand, and poked into the back of my head, round which the hair was gathered tight, and the whole tied around with a leather thong. When I was dressed for parade I could scarcely get my eyelids to perform their office; the skin of my eyes and face was drawn so tight by the plug... And to this an enormous high stock-collar was poked under my chin, so that I felt as if I had swallowed a ramrod. Shortly after... dinner was served, but my poor jaws refused to act... and when I made an attempt to eat, my pad went up and down like a sledge hammer.

War, and New Regiments

Captain Robert Jenkins was the captain of an English merchant ship which had been involved in a clash with the Spanish Navy patrolling in the seas near the Spanish colonies in the West Indies. The Spaniards had made many complaints about English attempts to smuggle goods into their colonies. On the English side there had been many stories of Spanish ships stopping and searching English vessels found in the seas around the West Indies. According to these stories, the Spaniards tortured English sailors and turned many of their ships adrift in the open seas. In 1738 Captain Jenkins returned home and told how

23 A soldier of the 34th Regiment of Foot in 1742. This was the stance taken at the command of 'Attention' before the 'Heels together' position was introduced. Notice the clumsy weapons, the awkward uniform and the unserviceable white gaiters.

24 A British Grenadier in 1780 with his powdered hair, decorated redcoat, thigh-length gaiters and useless headgear. It is not surprising that the American Indians and the American colonist-rebels found the British soldier an easy victim.

25 A bald-headed Captain Jenkins tries to show his ear to Sir Robert Walpole, who is unwilling to examine this latest example of Spanish attacks on British ships and seamen. One of Walpole's assistants (*on the right*) can be seen driving away a British merchant with his list of complaints against the Spaniards. In the end, however, Walpole had to give in to popular demand, and war was declared against Spain in 1739.

he had been tied to the mast and his ear ripped off. As proof of his story he brought his ear home — preserved in a bottle. Public opinion was outraged and forced Walpole to agree to a declaration of war against Spain in October 1739. This war is often referred to as the War of Jenkins's Ear, and it merged into a general European War which, off and on, lasted until 1763.

Throughout these years Britain's main enemy was France, allied to a now declining Spain. New regiments were required to go overseas and there must have been many who behaved as Henry Paget was to do when he heard about the declaration of war against France in 1793:

> The moment I heard it I jumped upon my horse and rode all night without stopping to Hertford Bridge. Here I dined and by chaise into London. I instantly wrote to Mr Pitt (the PM) to beg to see him ... I told him my anxiety to raise a Regiment of Cavalry. He told me Cavalry was not then wanted; that I might raise a Battalion of Infantry and have the rank of Lieut-Colonel. I instantly closed with him ... My father was put to great expense in raising the Regiment. Many commissions were given away, which in other hands would have been sold.

Indeed, many commissions were sold — purchasing of commissions remained common practice until the 1870s. One effect of this system was summed up by a Major-General Craig in a letter to the War Office:

> There is not a young man in the Army that cares ... whether his commanding officer approves of his conduct or not. His position depends not on their smiles or frowns — his friends can give him a thousand pounds and in a fortnight he becomes a captain. Out of the 125 regiments of cavalry and 26 of infantry which we have here, 21 are literally commanded by boys or idiots — I have had the curiosity to count them over.

The British soldier had to pay a heavy price for the incompetence of his superiors.

The Indian Empire

The struggle in India began as a struggle between the British and French trading companies there. But in 1740 this private struggle merged with the larger contest between Britain and France which was taking place in Europe and also in North America. Robert Clive had succeeded in defeating French ambitions in Madras in the 1740s but even more important was his conquest of Bengal in the 1750s, following which the British government took charge of the areas of India which had been conquered.

Later, in the 1790s, Sir Arthur Wellesley (later the Duke of Wellington) won fame as the commander of the army which defeated Tipoo Sahib, the Tiger of Mysore, an ally of the French and an enemy of Britain. Colonel Beatson has left us an account of various battles in which Wellesley's army defeated Tipoo's. In one:

> Two thousand of his French-trained troops advanced in column on the 33rd who held their fire with the utmost steadiness until the enemy were sixty yards away; then came the deadly British volleys tearing holes in the close-packed columns; confusion spread and the British cavalry easily scattered them.

Wellesley won many other battles — and more territory for Britain. Colin Campbell of the 78th was one of his officers. He wrote: 'The General was in the thick of the action the whole time. I never saw a man so cool as he was, though I can assure you till our troops got the order to advance the fate of the day seemed doubtful.'

Against France in Europe

Although the French and British were fighting their colonial wars in India and America, they were also engaged in a European war. At the Battle of Dettingen in 1743, King George II was the last British king actually to command his Army in the field. James Wolfe, then only 16 years old, took part in the battle; he wrote to his father:

> The cannons on both sides began to ply about till one o'clock in the morning, and we were exposed to the fire of them (said to be above fifty pieces) for near three hours, a great part of which planked us terribly from the other side of the water.

The packed masses of infantrymen had to stand up to the 'planking' or pounding from the enemy until the commander gave the order to march. Among the regiments at Dettingen were the Royal Welch Fusiliers who were attacked by the French cavalry. They came at them:

> at full trot with pistols in both hands and swords dangling by the wrist. Arrived within range they fired their pistols, dashed the empty weapons in the faces of the British and then fell to the sword, but the Fusiliers fought

like devils, their platoon-firing thundering out as regularly as on parade and the French horses fell back repulsed.

Finally, the Royal Welch advanced. As one of their officers wrote:

Our people imitated their predecessors in the last war gloriously, marching in close order, as firm as a wall and did not fire till we came within 60 paces, and still kept advancing; so that we had soon closed with the enemy, if they had not retreated: For when the smoke blew off a little, instead of being among their living, we found the dead in heaps about us; and the second fire turn'd them to the right about, and upon a long trot. We engaged two other Regiments afterwards who stood but one fire each; and their Blue French Foot Guards made the best of their way without firing a shot...Our Regiment sustain'd little loss, tho' much engaged; and indeed our whole Army gives us great honour...We have no more than 50 kill'd and wounded (and one Officer besides the Colonel). What preserved us, was our keeping close order, and advancing near the enemy ere we fir'd. Several that popp'd at 100 Paces lost more of their men and did less execution; for the French will stand fire at a distance, tho' 'tis plain they cannot look men in the face.

26 The 20th Regiment (later the Lancashire Fusiliers), armed just with pikes and muskets, repel a charge from the French cavalry at Minden, 1 August 1759. Notice the roses in the infantrymen's hats, the regimental band coming just behind the lines of infantrymen, and the commander sitting on horseback from where he can see the whole battlefield.

27 The death of General Wolfe at the siege of Quebec, 1759. Wolfe was only 30 years old when he was appointed commanding officer of the British troops fighting the French in Canada. He died as his men were about to succeed in their attack upon the important stronghold of Quebec.

This great victory was surpassed by the most impressive victory at Minden in 1759, when three lines of French cavalry were broken by the British infantry, who then repulsed a counter attack by French infantry and routed the enemy. Since then, all the regiments who took part in that battle (except the Royal Welch) have worn roses on their headdress on August 1st (Minden Day) in memory of the troops who, on their way to the battle, stopped near a rose garden and picked roses with which they decorated their hats.

America
The French had set up a number of fortified posts along the River Ohio in America. The most important of these was named Fort Duquesne after the French military commander. In 1755 General Braddock led a British force from Virginia on a march to Fort Duquesne. About nine miles (14 km) from the fort he was ambushed by Indians commanded by French officers. The British force, in redcoats, powdered pigtails, white gaiters, marched straight forward in columns as if on a parade ground. As the ambushers fired, the British ran for cover and returned the fire from behind the trees. Braddock and his officers ordered their men out of their 'skulking holes' back into their columns, where they were slaughtered. Braddock himself died — another leader unworthy of the men he commanded.

However, in 1759, with William Pitt as the Minister in charge of the wars against France, General Forbes was commander of a British force sent to attack Fort Duquesne. On 6 September 1758 he wrote to Pitt:

> My advanced post consisting of 1,500 men are now in possession of a strong post 9 miles [14 km] on the other side of Laurel Hill, and about 40 from Duquesne, nor had the enemy ever suspected my attempting such a road till very lately, they having been all along securing the strong passes and fords of the rivers, upon General Braddock's route . . .
>
> I vainly at the beginning flattered myself that some very good service might be drawn from Virginia and Pennsylvania forces, but am sorry to find that a few of their principal officers excepted, all the rest are an extreme bad collection of broken innkeepers, horse jockeys and Indian traders . . .

> In a few days I shall have most of my troops in readiness of marching to the banks of the Ohio ... and if refused the food demanded from the Pennsylvanians I shall most certainly try it upon flour and rice, with the assistance of what live cattle we can carry forward with us.

Forbes was successful in his attack on the Fort; on 27 November 1758 he wrote again to Pitt:

> Sir,
> I do myself the honour of acquainting you that it has pleased God to crown His Majesty's Arms with success over all his enemies upon the Ohio, by my having obliged the enemy to burn and abandon Fort Duquesne.

Today Pittsburgh stands on the site of the old fort.

The Treatment of the Men
William Cobbett enlisted as a private in 1784. Writing about trying to live on 'a miserable sixpence a day', he said:

> Judge of the quantity of food to sustain life in a lad of 16, and to enable him to exercise with a musket [it weighed nearly 11 lb or 5 kg] six to eight hours a day ... I have seen them [his comrades] lay in their berths, many and many a time, actually crying on account of hunger. The whole week's food was not a bit too much for one day.

Few men received their sixpence (now 2½p) a day. In 1747 the commander-in-chief issued an order which said:

> The commander-in-chief being convinced that the weekly stoppages in the marching regiments of foot are of great benefit to the men, by enabling them to be provided with good shoes, gaiters, linen and other necessaries, and to serve as a fund for making good the too frequent waste of ammunition, and loss of arms and accoutrements through idleness and neglect, it is the commander-in-chief's orders, that the Foot Guards be put under the same regulation of stoppages.

The stoppage was 2½p a week for a private, up to 5p a week for a sergeant. Then until 1771, 5 per cent of the man's pay was deducted as a fee to the paymaster general and ½p a week deducted for the surgeon's pay. No wonder that men had little to spend on food or that they resorted to theft.

If found guilty of theft, not having his hair dressed properly, insubordination or any other 'crime', the soldier was punished in one or other savage manner. In 1717 minor offences were punished by branding on the forehead, cutting off of ears, or picketing, that is, men were hung by one wrist from a tree while they stood with a bare heel resting on a pointed stake. In 1750 a soldier was sentenced to be bored through the tongue because he had uttered a blasphemy.

In 1761 punishments which could be imposed by any officer, without a court martial, included tying together of the neck and heels, with one gun tied under the knees and another over the neck. The guns were then tied together so that the man had his chin between his knees until, as one officer wrote: 'blood gushed out of his nose, mouth and ears and some men suffered ruptures.'

Men were also forced to run the gauntlet of the regiment drawn up in rows facing inwards. The 'criminal' stripped to the waist, then walked through the ranks while each man lashed him. To make sure that he did not run, a sergeant walked in front of him holding a lance to his chest. This method of punishment was abandoned in 1805. So was the strappado in which the victim had his arms tied behind his back and was pulled up high by a system of pulleys before he was suddenly dropped with a jerk. This was repeated three or four times, usually ending with the victim's shoulder joints being dislocated.

The most common form of punishment — one not abandoned in the Army until 1881 — was flogging, in which a victim was tied to a triangle and lashed with the 'cat' — a whip which usually had six, but sometimes nine 'tails'. The tails were usually two feet (60 cm) long and tied in three large knots which would cause even more pain.

In 1807 the poet Robert Southey wrote:

The offender is sometimes sentenced to receive a thousand lashes — a surgeon stands by to feel his pulse during the execution and determine how long the flogging can continue without killing him. His wound, for from the shoulders to the loins it leaves him one wound, is dressed, and as soon as it is sufficiently healed to be laid open in the same manner, he is brought out to undergo the remainder of his sentence.

Some Progress

In 1804 General Maitland wrote: 'The progress of wealth and the application of productive labour must indispose the lower orders from entering into a military life.'

Having considered the pay, food, clothing and punishments offered to men it is not surprising that they did not rush to join the Army. In 1777, as an attraction, Chelsea Hospital took in some of the former servicemen, while ex-servicemen who could not get a place in the Hospital were paid an out-pension of £7.62p a year which, as one writer said in 1801 was:

Particularly in the North a comfortable provision for old age, which every man might obtain by twenty years' faithful service. But an injudicious piece of economy put in practice about 1777, has taken away much of its attraction; this was a general call [to fight] on all out-pensioners [old soldiers] whatsoever, without any exception to want of limbs, or extreme old age.

In 1786 the Prime Minister, Pitt the Younger, persuaded an unwilling Parliament to agree to the building of the first Army barracks; by 1805 there

28 Troops being used in 1780 to control rioting Londoners who were following Lord George Gordon's violent campaign against the government. One reason for the unpopularity of British soldiers was their behaviour at this time, described by the diarist, Fanny Burney, who wrote: 'much slaughter has been made by the military among the mob . . . it is impossible not to shudder at hearing of their destruction.'

were 203 barracks in existence. However, conditions in the barracks were deplorable. Cavalry had to live 8 to a room, infantry 12 to a room. One roller towel was all that was issued weekly to each room; men slept two to a bed — a practice which Wellington tried to stop by issuing men with hammocks. He wrote: 'The beastly practice of two great hulking fellows stark naked sleeping together must be done away with.'

Public Opinion

In general the public feared the Army. Some believed that a large, standing, professional Army might be used by the government to overawe the people — which was why James II had been driven from the throne. Others feared the Army because of the behaviour of many of the men. In 1779 *The Times* reported:

> Last week the Volunteers . . . marched into this town . . . on their routes to the grand depot, at Horsham. The large bounties which these men have received enable them to keep up a scene of drunkenness . . . which it is very difficult to restrain. After parade here on Saturday evening, Sir Joseph Mawbey, and other Officers . . . were compelled to have recourse to their drawn swords, to enforce order.

6. Wellington's Army, 1800-1815

In February 1793 war broke out between Britain and the revolutionary government of France. This was to last for 22 years with only two short periods of peace. A contemporary account of the Army tells us that in 1793:

> Our Army was lax in its discipline, entirely without system, and very weak in number. Each colonel of a regiment managed it according to his own notions, or neglected it altogether; professional pride was rare; professional knowledge still more so. Never was a kingdom less prepared for a stern and arduous conflict.

The Army Leaders

Why was the Army so badly trained and its organization so poor? One reason was that successive governments refused to spend enough money on an Army which was unpopular with the taxpayers. Another reason was the poor quality of most of the Army's leaders. There were, of course, the exceptions, but a system which allowed a man to buy a commission for as little as £450, and to buy a whole regiment for £5,000, did not naturally bring the best leaders to the front — it only brought the richest to command.

The Army which went to Flanders in 1793 was commanded by the Duke of York. His incompetent leadership ensured that about 10,000 men had died, or were severely disabled by sickness and neglect, by the time they returned home in 1795.

But the Duke was conscious of some, at least, of the Army's failings, and on his return he issued orders which were intended to improve the quality of officers. Army officers were no longer allowed to go on leave whenever they wished but would, in future, have to apply for leave. Each officer had to make confidential reports on his fellow officers, and no-one was allowed to hold a command in the field without having had some previous experience. No-one could buy the commission of major (or above) without having served in a lower rank for at least six years.

Outstanding Army leaders included Sir Ralph Abercromby, who led the Army in the Egyptian campaign and died in 1801, and Sir John Moore who commanded the Army in the Spanish Peninsula until his death at Corunna. Sir Arthur Wellesley, later the Duke of Wellington, took over after Moore's death and led the Army in a series of great victories in Portugal and Spain. It was Wellington who later led the allied forces in the Battle of Waterloo, 1815, which brought Napoleon's reign to an end.

29 The Battle of Assaye, 23 September 1803. In this battle, Sir Arthur Wellesley (later the Duke of Wellington) led British troops against the Mahratta army. Notice how even in the heat of India the British soldiers had to have powdered hair, white breeches, a red coat, a decorated hat — they looked 'pretty' but were overburdened by much useless dress.

Wellington's Soldiers

Wellington made no effort to make himself popular with his soldiers as Sir John Moore had done. He described his Peninsula Army as: 'The scum of the earth and it is really wonderful that we should have made them the fine fellows they are.' In his *Eventful Life of a Soldier* Joseph Donaldson tried to explain why he and his fellow soldiers sometimes behaved as though they were 'the scum' that Wellington spoke about:

> The soldier . . . was one of the veriest slaves existing, obliged to rise two or three hours before day to commence his cleaning operations. His hair required to be soaped, floured, frizzed, or tortured into some uncouth shape which gave him acute pain . . . He had his musket to burnish, his cap and cartridge box to polish with heel-ball, and his white breeches to pipe-clay, so that it generally required three or four hours' hard labour to prepare him for parade; and when he turned out, he was like something made of glass, which the slightest accident might derange or break to pieces. He was then subjected to a rigid inspection, in which, if a single hair stood out of its place, extra guard, drill, or some other punishment, awaited him. When to this was added the supercilious tyrannical demeanour of his superiors, who seemed to look upon him as a brute animal who had neither soul nor feeling, and who caned or flogged him without mercy for the slightest offence, we cannot wonder that he became the debased being, in body and mind, which they already considered him.

In 1798 the men had been given an increase in pay — a daily bread allowance of ½p a day — and they could use this to supplement their daily rations which, in the Peninsula, were (per week) a pound of meat, a pound of bread, a pint of wine or a third of a pint of whisky. Rations sometimes arrived just as the men were due to march off, so that the hacked-off lump of meat, still dripping with blood, had to be stuffed with the bread into the haversack where the two became a horrible mash.

The private soldier's pay was increased in 1798 to 5p a day — and it remained at this level until 1891. But pay was often weeks or months in arrears because the departments responsible for paying soldiers were usually corrupt and inefficient. The soldier could buy little or no comfort for himself, and the Army certainly provided him with none — for the first four years in the Peninsula they had no tents. Meanwhile, an officer might have as many as a dozen horses to carry his gear, which often included dressing tables and easy chairs.

Losses

The inefficient and corrupt supply system meant that the men received a poor service. On 21 August 1809 Wellington wrote:

> The distress for want of provisions, and its effects, have at last obliged me to move towards the frontiers of Portugal in order to refresh my troops... Since the 22nd of last month, when the Spanish and British armies joined, the troops have not received ten days' bread; on some days they have received nothing; and for many days together only meat without salt; frequently flour instead of bread, and scarcely ever more than one third, or at most half, of a ration... The sickness of the army has increased considerably... Indeed, there are few, if any, officers or soldiers of the army who, although doing their duty, are not more or less affected by dysentery, and the whole lie out, and nothing can be got for them in this part of the country.

On their long marches, wrote an officer, 'I have often seen the blood soaking through the gaiters, and over the heels of the soldiers' hardshoes, whitened with the dust.' Many men dropped out because they had no shoes; they walked along the softer verges, their feet cut into a bloody mess, bruised by stones, sticks and thorns. When a man was wounded he lay in the field until he died, or walked until he could find a doctor. But sometimes the doctors were overwhelmed. Sir Charles Bell wrote home after Waterloo:

> At six o'clock I took the knife in my hand and continued incessantly at work till seven in the evening; and so the second day, and again the third

30 The Battle of Talavera, 27-28 July 1809. This battle, wrote Wellesley, was 'a most desperate one. But we maintained our positions and gave the French a terrific beating.' After the battle, Wellesley was given the title Viscount Wellington of Talavera. Notice the close-packed ranks of infantrymen advancing, and the presence of the officers on a hill from where they can overlook the whole scene and direct operations.

31 Wellington had an army of about 60,000 in the Peninsula, behind a series of fortifications which stretched from the River Tagus to the sea. This army could be supplied and reinforced from the sea where the British ruled supreme. As a result the British officers felt very secure, and shot and hunted as they would have done on their estates in Britain. In March 1811 the French were forced to retreat — because of shortage of supplies and provisions. Wellington then led his army out and harried their retreat.

day. All the decencies of performing surgical operations were soon neglected. While I amputated one man's thigh, there lay at one time thirteen all beseeching to be taken next. It was a strange thing to feel my clothes stiff with blood, and my arms powerless with the exertion of using the knife... After being eight days among the wounded, I visited the field of battle... But there must ever be associated with the honours of Waterloo to my eyes, the most shocking signs of woe; to my ear, accents of entreaty; outcry from the manly breast, interrupted forcible expressions of the dying and noisome smells.

On the March

Wellington had taught his Indian Army how to march — sometimes as much as 40 miles (60 km) a day. On one occasion he marched his men for 60 miles (96 km) in less than thirty hours, including a ten-hour rest period. In the Peninsula War, his men had to get used to long marches. The Rifle Brigade for example marched 52 miles (84 km) in twenty-four hours to take part in the Battle of

Talavera. For Wellington and the officers this was not such a great hardship — they had their horses and their gear was carried in wagons. But Rifleman Harris was convinced that the long marches were a great hardship because of:

> ... the infernal load we carried on our backs. The weight I myself toiled under was tremendous, and I often wonder at the strength I possessed at this period, which enabled me to endure it; for, indeed, I am convinced that many of our infantry sank and died under the weight of their knapsacks alone. For my own part, I marched under a weight sufficient to impede the free motions of a donkey; for besides my well-filled kit, there was the greatcoat rolled on its top, my blanket and camp kettle, my haversack, stuffed full of leather for repairing the men's shoes, together with a hammer and other tools (the lapstone I took the liberty of flinging to the devil), ship-biscuit and beef for three days. I also carried my canteen filled with water, my hatchet and rifle, and eighty rounds of ball cartridge in my pouch.

After a long march, burdened as they were, the soldiers were then flung into battle — perhaps against a fortress or maybe against an enemy line of infantry and cavalry. It is not really surprising that sometimes the men behaved cruelly to the conquered town or defeated enemy. At Badajoz, for example, it was noted:

> The infuriated soldiery resembled rather a pack of hell-hounds vomited up from the infernal regions for the extirpation of mankind than what they were twelve short hours previously — well-organized, brave, disciplined and obedient British Army, and burning only with impatience for what is called glory.

32 The survivors of the Battle of Albuhera, 1812. This tribute to the 'diehards' was painted by Lady Butler.

33 Wellington with some of his men during the crossing of the Pyrénées, July 1813.

Whatever accounts may be given of the horrors which attended and immediately followed the storming of Badajoz, they must fall far short of the truth... it is impossible to imagine them... The frenzied military mob... were ferociously employed in indiscriminate carnage, universal plunder and devastation of every kind... I beheld the savages tear the rings from the ears of beautiful women who were their victims, and when the rings could not be immediately removed from their fingers with the hand, they tore them off with their teeth ... The sack continued for three days without intermission; each day I witnessed its horrid and abominable effects ... I shrink from further description.

The success of the Army depended in part on the quality of its leaders. But in a large part it also depended on the courage of the men. Stocqueler tells of a trooper, Wilson:

I saw him engaged hand to hand with a French dragoon; I saw him ... give and receive more than one pass, with equal skill and courage. Just then a French officer delivered a thrust at poor Harry Wilson's body, and delivered it effectually. I firmly believe that Wilson died on the instant; yet, though he felt the sword in its progress, he, with characteristic self-command, kept his eye still on the enemy in his front, and raising himself in his stirrups, let fall upon the Frenchman's helmet such a blow that the brass and skull parted before it, and the man's head was cloven asunder to the chin.

Men had to stand up to the sort of artillery attack described by one officer who was at Waterloo:

We recommenced firing at the enemy's masses, and the cannonade, spreading, soon became general again along the line. Whilst thus occupied with our front, we suddenly became sensible of a most destructive flanking fire from a battery which had come, the Lord knows how, and established itself on a knoll somewhat higher than the ground we stood on, and only about 400 or 500 yards [about 400 m] a little in advance of our left flank. The rapidity and precision of this fire were quite appalling.

After such an attack they then had to face an attack from an infantry line as Captain Powell of the First Foot Guards described:

The Emperor [Napoleon] was so much pressed by the Prussian advance on his right that he determined to make a last grand effort ... His Artillery were ordered to concentrate their whole fire on the intended point of attack. That point was the rise of our position about half-way between Hougoumont and La Haye Sainte. ... The firing ceased, and as the smoke cleared away a most superb sight opened on us. A close column of Grenadiers ... of la Moyenne Garde, about 6,000 strong, led by Marshal Ney, were seen ascending the rise shouting 'Vive l'Empereur!' They continued to advance till within fifty or sixty paces of our front, when the Brigade were ordered to stand up. Whether it was from the sudden and unexpected appearance of a Corps so near them or the tremendous heavy fire we threw into them, la Garde, who had never before failed in an attack suddenly stopped. Those who from a distance could see the affair, tell us that the effect of our fire seemed to force the head of the Column bodily back.

34 'Chelsea Pensioners reading the Waterloo Despatch', a painting by Sir David Wilkie, 1822. Wellington had asked the artist to paint a picture of the pensioners at the Hospital. Wilkie added the Despatch to his picture in order to add some importance to the painting and as a tribute to Wellington's great victory.

Perhaps the greatest tribute to the British Army, though, came from Marshal Soult who had been defeated by Wellington at the Battle of Albuhera in 1812:

There is no beating these troops, in spite of their generals. I always thought they were bad soldiers; now I am sure of it. I had turned their right, pierced their centre and everywhere victory was mine, but they did not know how to run.

7. The Queen's Army, 1840-80

Burma

Throughout the nineteenth century the history of the British Army is the history of the expansion of the British Empire – on which 'the sun never set' but across which the soldiers' feet continually tramped. Between 1824 and 1826 British and Indian soldiers were involved in the First Burmese War. The Burmese were easy enemies and only 166 men were killed in the capture of Rangoon, while none at all were killed at Arakan. But the Army's greatest enemy – disease – was very active. In the Army hospital in Rangoon 3,160 men died, and 595 died in the hospital at Arakan. Scurvy, cholera and malaria were the main diseases that attacked the Army – which was unprepared for such attacks. Poor food, lack of medical equipment and personnel, inadequate clothing and lack of intelligent leadership, allowed the diseases to flourish.

35 A combined naval and military landing in Burma, 27 March 1825. Notice the disciplined formation of the infantrymen (*foreground*), the Burmese ships on the right as you look at the picture and the pieces of cannon on the left.

Afghanistan

In 1838 a British Army entered Afghanistan to support a friendly ruler. In November 1841 an Afghan leader, Dost Mohammed, led a rebellion against the British attempt to take over his country. The British were led by General Elphinstone, whose headquarters were at Kabul.

After consultation he agreed to withdraw his Army, and in January 1842 the 44th Regiment (the Essex) led 4,500 troops (mostly Indian), British women and children, and 12,000 Indian servants and camp followers, out of Kabul. The force had to get back to British India via the Khyber Pass, then under two metres of snow. Afghan tribesmen attacked the column — and within four days 9,000 people had been killed by the Afghans or by frostbite. By 14 January there were only 65 men left, and at Gundamuck they defied the Afghans; when their ammunition ran out they fought with swords and bayonets. Captain Soutar wrapped the Regimental Colours around his waist — and when he was captured, wounded, by the Afghans they thought him a valuable prisoner to be

36 Dr Brydon arriving at Jellalabad (1842), the only survivor of the proud British army which had left Kabul just a few weeks earlier. This painting by Lady Butler is entitled 'The Remnants of an Army'.

held for ransom. Dr Brydon, the only survivor, made his way to Jellalabad where the 13th Regiment (the Somerset) formed the garrison. The town was besieged by Afghans for over three months before relief arrived.

Later, an expedition was sent to attack Dost Mohammed and the Regimental Colour of the 44th was found and brought back to England where it now hangs in the Chapel at Warley.

Sikh Wars

During the 1840s the British Army in India was fighting against the Sikhs of the Sind district. The Sikhs were well-armed, well-led, and very brave. They attacked the British headquarters at Delhi in December 1845. Sir Henry Gough led his Army to attack the Sikhs at Ferozepore and the Sikhs not only repelled the attacks but seemed likely to mount a successful counter-attack against the British. They owed their apparent success to their efficient gunnery. William Hodson wrote:

> The 80th is a splendid corps; well-behaved in cantonments and first-rate in action. I lay [near] them on the memorable night when Lord Hardinge called out: 'Eightieth, that gun must be silenced!' They jumped up, advanced through the darkness, and soon we lost the tread of their feet while they gradually gained the front of the enemy's battery whose fire had caused so much loss; when suddenly we saw the blaze of the Sikh battery, followed at once by a thrilling cheer from the 80th... In a few moments they moved back silently but they had left 45 of their number and two captains to mark the exploit by their graves.

General Hardinge, commander of the force, wrote: 'I found myself with... that Regiment which has earned for itself immortal fame in the annals of the British Army — Her Majesty's 80th Regiment... The British Infantry as usual carried the day.'

Soldiers Abroad

But military life was not all glory and success. Corporal Ryder of the 32nd described a march under Indian conditions:

> We struck camp at 11 o'clock. This was a very long day's march, over sandy deserts and plains, the water being short and the horrors past describing. We drew near to a well some time in the morning, and the confusion all round was fearful — the men rushing and pushing to get at it, some letting their caps fall into it, and some their bayonets; one poor fellow had fallen, and was begging that someone would give him a draught to save his life; but, God help him! He spent his breath in vain. The doctor seeing him in this deplorable state, asked a man to give him a drink, but was refused.

And while some officers were efficient, too many of them — wealthy buyers of commissions that they did not deserve — were incompetent. And while the

37 Troops on the march through the heat and dust of India, 1858.

stories of the men's bravery are true, it is also true that too many men were undisciplined. Perhaps there are excuses for them — poorly-led and badly-fed, exposed to intense heat and sometimes to intense cold; poorly-paid and badly-housed — it is not altogether surprising that men misbehaved. Punishments in India, as elsewhere, were barbarous. Lashings were common while executions were not rare. Sergeant MacMullen was at a military execution in 1844:

> All the troops at the station were drawn up to form three sides of a square, the gallows occupying the centre of the vacant side . . . A guard proceeded to the criminal's cell, who was dressed in a white gown and placed in a dooly [litter] and borne to the left flank of the troops. First went the band, playing the 'Dead March', next a portion of the guard followed by four soldiers bearing a coffin. After these came the criminal, the rear was brought up by the remainder of the guard . . . The procession moved slowly alongside the square, till it reached the gallows, at the foot of which the coffin was placed. The criminal, left alone with his guard and executioner, now mounted the platform. The rope was adjusted round his neck. 'Mother, mother!' . . . The next moment the drop fell, and he was swinging in mid-air.

The Army was also active in various parts of Africa. There was a succession of Ashanti Wars and Zulu Wars as the British extended their Empire northwards from the Cape of Good Hope. This meant that, for the soldier, there was much travelling between Britain and various parts of the world. What was it like in a nineteenth-century troopship? Mrs Sherwood, the wife of a captain in the 53rd Regiment, spent four months en route to India:

Our cabin was just the width of a gun over which the cot was slung. On entering the cabin, which was formed only of canvas, we were forced to stoop under, there not being one foot from the head or the foot of the cot to the partition . . . We were in constant darkness and we have much putrid water on board.

John Shipp also described a voyage to India:

. . . the scurvy broke out among us in a most frightful manner. Scarcely a single individual escaped. The dying were burying the dead . . . the pestilence baffled the aid of medicine and the skill of the medical attendants. My poor legs were as big as drums; my gums swollen to an enormous size; my tongue too big for my mouth; and all I could eat was raw potatoes and vinegar.

38 The Indian Mutiny, 1857. The destruction of a bungalow at Meerut.

Who Joined the Army?

When we look at the way in which men were treated, the wonder is that anyone joined the Army. Sergeant MacMullen made a survey of why men joined the Army in the 1840s, and published it in *Camp and Barrack Room*:

Indigent — Embracing labourers and mechanics out of employ and who merely seek for support	80 in 120
Indigent — Respectable persons induced by misfortune or imprudence	2 in 120
Idle — Who consider a soldier's life is an easy one	16 in 120
Bad characters — Who fall back upon the army as a last resource	8 in 120
Criminals — Who seek to escape from the consequence of their offences	1 in 120
Perverse sons — Who seek to grieve their parents	2 in 120
Discontented and restless	8 in 120
Ambitious	1 in 120
Others	2 in 120

The Crimea

And so, in 1853, a well-dressed but poorly-led Army was sent by the politicians to fight against the Russians who were trying to capture Constantinople. The officers' attitudes may be illustrated by two stories. Alexis Soyer, a London chef, proposed a new system of cooking (on a stove called after him), and an improved diet for soldiers. But General Eyre dismissed Soyer's ideas with: 'Soldiers don't require such good messes as these while campaigning. You will improve the cook but spoil the soldier.'

The other story concerns Lord Cardigan. There was a request to move a troop of horses from muddy slush to dry ground — but Cardigan refused to allow the men to leave the filthy and dangerous lines because, as he said, 'To move the lines would spoil the pattern of the whole Army's symmetry.'

Private Robert Browning of the 17th arrived at Balaclava in November 1854, and wrote:

> ... in our tent alone we were reduced from 19 down to 8 in the first three months by those companions of active service — exhaustion and disease — for it was no unusual sight in the morning to see the dead bodies of two or three men taken out from the tents, the men having passed away during the

39 'A Wellington Boot, or the Head of the Army', 1827. In 1817, a writer, Moncrief, made the first printed reference to Wellington boots. In this cartoon Wellington's head is shown sticking out of one. Wellington had his headquarters at Horse Guards Parade (*on the right*) and from there he vigorously opposed any proposals to reform the Army. His attitude contributed to the disasters of the Crimea.

night . . . Chocolate used to be sent out to us . . . in shape something like a big flat cheese. This chocolate we found would burn. We would set fire to it, place our canteen on the top and then wait for something warm; this being the only way we succeeded in doing so for the first few months.

. . . The rifle with which we had to defend ourselves was not like the modern magazine rifle, but the old-fashioned 'Brown Bess' with round bullet, the charge having to be rammed home in the rifle with the ramrod. Many a night when our duty and need for the rifle came, it was found impossible to use it, the ramrod being frozen to the rifle and quite immovable, the bayonet and butt end of the rifle having then to be brought into use.

A good deal of the blame for the disasters of the Crimean campaign must be laid at the door of the politicians and military leaders. The politicians were responsible for the inadequate supply system, the almost complete absence of medical services until Florence Nightingale's arrival, and for trying to ignore the

40 The Battle of Inkerman, 5 November 1854. Fewer than 8,000 British troops resisted the onslaught of 50,000 Russians. One historian wrote: 'Never in history, not even at Albuhera, did British soldiers fight with more bravery.' Notice the changed hair styles and headgear, the use of the rifle as a club, and the presence of the officer at the scene of the battle.

41 The Charge of the Light Brigade, 1854. 'Into the valley of death rode the six hundred', wrote Tennyson later of their brave but futile gesture.

complaints of critics such as *The Times* war correspondent William Howard Russell, whose articles eventually forced the government to send out Miss Nightingale and 38 nurses to look after the wounded in the hospital at Scutari. It was the politicians and their civil servants who tried to prevent Miss Nightingale from getting the supplies she needed, and from installing a proper system of drainage.

But the officers must share the blame for the disasters of the Crimea. There were any number of brave officers. For example, Sir George Brown, 'conspicuous on a grey horse, rode in front of his Light Division, urging them with voice and gesture. Gallant fellows! They were worthy of such a gallant chief.'

But there were also the officers who thought more of social position, their own advancement and public esteem than they did of their men. Henry Clifford won a Victoria Cross at the Battle of Inkerman. He explained the Charge of the Light Brigade:

> Little confidence has been placed in the commanding powers of Lord Lucan commanding the Cavalry, and long have been the feuds between His Lordship and Lord Cardigan who commands the Light Brigade; and it was thought if a verbal order was sent to Lord Lucan it might be misunderstood,

or not carried out. A written order was, therefore, sent from Lord Raglan by Captain Nolan ... desiring his Lordship 'To charge!' 'To charge what?' said Lord Lucan very naturally. 'Here are your orders,' said poor Nolan, pointing to the paper, 'and there', pointing to the Russian Army, 'is the enemy', and shouting 'Come on' to the Light Brigade of Cavalry, he dashed forward. He was wrong in doing so and his conduct was most insulting to Lord Lucan and Lord Cardigan, who at the head of his Brigade, pale with indignation, shouted to him to stop but ... a shell struck him in the chest, and in a few minutes he was a mangled corpse. Lord Lucan then ordered the Light Brigade of Cavalry between 600 and 700 to charge the Russian Army, 30,000 strong.

Reforming the Army
The disasters of the Crimean War forced the politicians to take a close look at the Army — its officers, its organization, its supply and medical services as well as military questions of training and equipment.

The task of reforming the Army fell to Edward Cardwell, who became Secretary of State for War in 1868. He abolished the system of purchasing commissions, by which, in 1856, a man had to pay £2,400 for promotion to captain and £7,000 to become a lieutenant. Cardwell set aside £7 million as compensation to men who had purchased their commissions and would not now be able to sell them. But this was a small price to pay for ending a system by which a rich incompetent could have men's lives in his hands. In future, promotion would depend on merit and not on wealth.

Cardwell tried to improve life for the ordinary soldier. He abolished the system by which a man signed on to serve for life — and substituted a system of short service by which a man could sign on for 12 years, 6 of which he spent with the Army and 6 of which he spent in the Army Reserve. He tried to make life in the Army a more attractive prospect for a better quality of soldier by abolishing flogging, arranging for the dismissal of people found guilty of serious crimes, increasing pay, and setting up a pension scheme for the ordinary soldier. However, politicians refused to make the Army too attractive; the rates of pay were still lower than those that could be earned outside, so that Army recruitment still depended on the economic situation. If the economy was booming and men could get good jobs and decent wages, then they did not join the Army; if the economy went into a depression so that there were few good jobs and lower wages, then men joined the Army. 'Jack Frost [or hunger] is our best recruiting officer,' said one officer.

Cardwell also tried to make the Army more efficient. He set up the Army Medical Service and started to build a number of Army hospitals. Training camps were established and special factories opened to ensure that the Army was supplied with enough efficient weapons. Schools of gunnery and musketry were also started to ensure that the men knew how to use the latest weapons.

Finally, Cardwell gave each regiment a territorial link with one English county. This ended the system of numbering each regiment, which many regretted. But it did give each regiment an appeal to a particular part of the

42 The Royal Sussex Regiment's Museum, part of Chichester City Museum. All regiments have a museum where they keep alive the memories of past greatness and so help to hand on to new recruits the regimental traditions.

country — Middlesex, Kent, Warwickshire or whatever — and it was hoped that the county would then become the natural recruiting ground for the regiment. This system also gave each regiment a natural Headquarters — in the county — where it could build its barracks, its museum and chapel, and from which it could organize its training. Each regiment was divided into two linked battalions, one of which was to serve abroad while the other served at home — in this way it was hoped that no regiment would ever again be sent abroad and then 'forgotten'.

Cardwell's reforms were not finalized until the 1880s by which time he was no longer in office. The reformed Army was expected to guard Britain against the danger of foreign invasion, garrison the many posts in the expanding Empire, and play a part in enlarging that Empire. As a music-hall song of the 1870s went:

> We don't want to fight but by jingo if we do,
> We've got the ships, we've got the men,
> And we've got the money too.
> We've fought the bear before, and while we're Britons true
> The Russians shall not have Constantinople.

8. The Popular Army, 1880-1914

The Recruits
In 1877 William Robertson, aged 17, joined the 16th Lancers. He wrote:

> Regiments were still composed mainly of old soldiers who, although very admirable comrades in some respects... were in many cases addicted to rough behaviour, heavy drinking, and hard swearing. They could not well be blamed for this. Year in and year out they went through the same routine, were treated like machines — lived only for the present, the single bright spot in their existence being the receipt of a few shillings — perhaps not more than one — on the weekly pay-day... These rugged veterans exacted full deference from the recruit, who was assigned the worst bed in the room, given the smallest amount of food and the least palatable, and was expected to share with them at the regimental canteen such cash as he might have in the purchase of beer sold at 3d a quart.

In the 1890s an Army chaplain wrote:

> When trade is bad we get good recruits and when good, bad ones. The Army is still recruited mainly from the class of manual labour. Men enlist for the queerest reasons... Once a patient in a military hospital told me he did so in order to have a military funeral, an honour that the poor fellow soon obtained. Another man gave to me as his reason for enlisting that he wanted to learn to read... He grew up quite illiterate and thought he would learn something quietly in a military school. Only 49 recruits in a thousand can be described as well educated.

The Lack of Initiative
But men who are constantly told that they are stupid and always treated as if they were machines will soon learn to live down to the low expectations which their commanders have of them. An outside observer, Stocqueler, had noted during the Crimean War:

> With all their courage and energy in action most of them were in some respects very helpless fellows. Few of them could handle a spade, fewer still an axe or a saw, a hammer or a trowel; they were bad cooks, and all, except the old soldiers, bad hands even at lighting a fire... A part of the sufferings of the British Army in the Crimea arose from this.

Archibald Forbes was a soldier who later became a war correspondent. He

43 Boers manning their trenches outside Mafeking. The besieged British inside the town could see the Boers with the help of binoculars. The scrubland between the Boers and the town was 'like a worn-out coconut matting' through which a Boer could creep up unseen. Notice the Boers' lack of spectacular uniforms.

followed the British Army on many campaigns and he noted that the British soldier was less able than the German and French soldiers of the 1890s:

> Today's soldier is tried by a much higher test than in the old close-quarter days... he often fails in the higher morals which his wider scope of individuality exacts of him if he is to be efficient. The officer gives the forward signal but the consequences of not obeying it do not come home with such swift vividness to the reluctant individual man. He is behind cover... how dear that cover is! So he lies still and his own particular wave goes on and leaves him behind. He may join the next or he may continue to lie still.

One effect of this lack of ability was that the British soldiers suffered at the hands of the Zulus at the Massacre of Isandlwana (1879), and at the hands of the Boers at the Battle of Majuba Hill (1881). Forbes wrote that the defeat at

44 British troops meeting a Boer rush on Spion Kop. Although the British soldier here has a khaki coloured uniform instead of the old redcoat, he is still weighted down by the equipment on his back. For him little has changed.

Majuba was due to the British soldier being 'so much a creature of cover and of dodging that he went all abroad when he saw a real live enemy standing up in front of him at point-blank range ... the Boer had better nerve.'

Kipling's Army and its Boots
In spite of the poor quality of the recruits and the incompetence of many officers, the British Army still marched its way through war after war in Asia and Africa. In 1880 Sir Donald Stewart led 7,000 men into battle in

Afghanistan; after a victory at Ahmed Khel he left 4,000 men behind at Kandahar while he marched on to Kabul; 2,500 men were sent from Kandahar under General Burrows to meet an enemy force of 10,000 Afghans who were better-equipped and better-led. After a long battle the British troops were forced into a triangular shape around which the enemy ran in their masses — some on foot, others on horseback. The 66th Foot (Berkshires) retreated to Maiwand where their commander was killed; the others fought until there were only eleven men left. Then, amazingly, the eleven charged the whole huge Afghan army — and the mass retreated, but picked off the British one by one. The Afghans chased the remainder of the Brigade to Kandahar but the delay caused by the 66th had given enough time for the rest to escape.

In August 1880 a force of 10,000 troops led by Sir Frederick Roberts marched about 350 miles from Kabul to Kandahar, to relieve the garrison there. In spite of the heat, and the lack of water and of sleep, the men covered the distance in 23 days. Immediately on arrival they gave battle, and scattered the Afghan forces. Robert's ability made him a popular hero:

> "'E's the man that done us well,
> An' we'll follow him to 'ell —
>   Won't we, Bobs?"

Popular Heroes
Roberts was a small Irishman whose success in Afghanistan caught the public imagination. In the 1870s and 1880s Britain began to be affected by a tide of imperialism; politicians such as Joseph Chamberlain swam to power on that tide, while politicians who tried to stem the tide — such as Gladstone — became unpopular.

The Sudan was part of the Egyptian Empire and when a revolt broke out there against the unpopular Egyptian government, Gladstone was unwilling to do as that government wished — namely to send an army to put down the revolt. Instead he sent General Gordon to the Sudanese capital, Khartoum, with orders to bring out the few British civil servants, traders, soldiers and their families. The following extract is from Gordon's *Journals:*

September 19 I did not escape with Stewart simply because the people would not have been such fools as to have let me go . . . I own to having been very insubordinate to Her Majesty's Government . . .
December 12-13 Small church parade . . . The Arabs fired two shells at the Palace . . .
December 13 Today is the 276th day of our anxiety . . . If some effort is not made before ten days' time the town will fall. It is inexplicable, this delay. If the Expeditionary Forces have reached the river and met my steamers, one hundred men are all that we require, just to show themselves . . . Any expeditionary force that may come up comes up for the honour of England and England will be grateful.

Gordon's death at the hands of the rebels aroused the fury of the British people against Gladstone, who had refused to send an expeditionary force until it was too late. On the other hand, the leader of the force, Kitchener, became a popular hero when he defeated the rebels at Omdurman and recaptured Khartoum. Kitchener was given the title of Lord Kitchener of Khartoum. Like Roberts, he too became a popular hero.

The Ranker

But if the public welcomed their heroes, they continued to ignore the ordinary soldier; indeed, their treatment of the ranker was worse than that; they continued to treat him as a sort of leper. It is to Kipling's credit that he had the ability to express the ordinary soldier's anger:

> I went into a public 'ouse to get a pint of beer,
> The publican 'e up and sez: 'We serve no redcoats here';
> The girls be'ind the bar they laughed and giggled fit to die,
> I outs into the streets again an' to myself size I:
> Oh it's 'Tommy this, 'an Tommy that, an' Tommy go away;'
> But it's 'Thank you, Mister Atkins' when the band begins to play.
>
> I went into a theatre as sober as could be,
> They gave a drunk civilian room, but 'adn't none for me;
> They sent me to the gallery or round the music 'alls,
> But when it comes to fighting, Lord! they'll shove me in the stalls!
> For it's 'Tommy this, an' Tommy that, an' Tommy wait outside';
> But it's 'Special train for Atkins' when the trooper's on the tide.

Non-Heroic Officers

Sir Garnet Wolseley had seen the effect of poor officer leadership while he was commander in Egypt between 1882 and 1885:

> I have seen splendid battalions kept in the rear while others of inferior quality were sent to the front because the general commanding did not dare employ against the enemy a corps whose commanding officer was manifestly incompetent... I hold that it is criminal to hand over in action the lives of gallant soldiers to men who are deplorably ignorant of the elements of their profession... It is but right that the nation should expect that none but competent and properly educated officers should be selected for the position of lieutenant colonel.

Even in 1890 officers were allowed to spend as many as 250 days away from their regiment, spending their time in sport or travel, or — if they were really enterprising — as war correspondents, as did a young lieutenant, Winston Churchill, who reported on Kitchener's march to Khartoum, various campaigns on the North-West Frontier of India, and on the Boer War.

45 The Boers had succeeded in an attack on the Yorkshire Regiment whose officer and sergeant were killed; the men were retreating in disorder when a force from the New Zealand Mounted Rifles led by a Captain Madocks made a sudden attack on the Boers and helped to rally the dispirited British (January 1900).

One result of this lack of training and experience was that men were still badly-led when the Boer War broke out in 1899. The Boers (Dutch farmers) did not want the British to take over the Transvaal Republic in South Africa. Chamberlain and Rhodes represented the politicians and businessmen who were eager to get their hands on the newly-discovered diamond and gold mines inside the Transvaal. So a war against the Boers was manufactured and the British waited confidently for the news of its occupation and annexation.

But the badly-led British Army suffered a series of disasters. Dutch strong points — often on the top of small hills called kops or kopjes — were attacked by frontal assault, with results described by Winston Churchill in *My Early Life*:

> Buller now began his fourth attempt to relieve Ladysmith [and] got his army thoroughly clumped-up in the maze of hills and spurs beyond Colenso. In these unfavourable conditions, without any turning movement, he assaulted the long-prepared, deeply-entrenched Boer position before Pieters... It was four o'clock when the Irish Brigade began to toil up the steep side of what is now called Inniskilling Hill, and sunset approached before the assault was delivered by the Inniskilling and Dublin Fusiliers. The

46 Hampstead rejoicing over the Relief of Mafeking (1900). For seven months (217 days) the British troops, led by Baden-Powell, had held out against the Boers. The relief of the town led to hysterical scenes in Britain — people at home welcomed some good news after the series of defeats the country had suffered at the hands of the Boers.

spectacle was tragic. Through our glasses we could see the Boers' heads and slouch hats in miniature silhouette, wreathed and obscured by shell-bursts, against the evening sky. Up the bare grassy slopes slowly climbed the brown figures and glinting bayonets of the Irishmen, and the rattle of intense musketry drummed in our ears. The climbing figures dwindled; they ceased to move; they vanished into the darkening hillside. Out of twelve hundred men who assaulted, both colonels, three majors, twenty officers and six hundred soldiers had fallen killed or wounded. The repulse was complete.

What remained of the Army was then attacked by that age-old enemy — disease. There is some dispute about the figures; the official history of the Boer War says that 7,792 men were killed in action while 13,250 were killed by disease; other authorities report that about 6,000 men were killed in action while 16,000 died from disease — the Army was even too inefficient to count its dead, let alone look after its wounded and sick.

Haldane's Reforms
The Boer War finally ended in victory after large reinforcements drawn from Canada and Australia, India and Egypt, and led by Roberts and Kitchener, were sent out there in 1900. Ladysmith, Kimberley and Mafeking were relieved — to the frenzied delight of a war-crazy British people.

But more practical politicians realized that there was little cause for rejoicing. What would have happened if Germany had used its growing power to help the Boers? What would happen if Britain ever had to face France or Russia or Germany in a major war? The Army which found it so difficult to defeat the tiny force of Boers would certainly be unable to defend the country's wealth and Empire against a strong nation.

The result was that the Liberals who came to power in 1906 set in train another major reform of the Army, comparable only to the changes made by Cardwell. R E Haldane was the Minister in charge of these reforms. He tried to make life better for the ordinary soldier by increasing pay, improving housing conditions and by such simple means as installing hot baths in barracks. New dining halls were built and so were libraries, reading and writing rooms. Haldane also tried to push through reforms in the training of the ordinary soldier. But most officers agreed with Colonel Henderson, who wrote in 1903:

The idea of transforming the Militia and Volunteers into an army of marksmen, capable of coping with the picked infantry of the Continent, is a vain dream. Marksmanship in a great mass of men depends on discipline and not on patriotism, and to believe that a large mass of men will become efficient soldiers, except under compulsion, is to disregard human nature.

Haldane also set up the Territorial Army which was intended to act as a sort of Army reserve in which volunteers would receive some Army training while still remaining civilians. By 1914 there were 14 Territorial Divisions and 14 mounted brigades. These formed a possible back-up force to the regular Army of six infantry divisions and one cavalry division. Each battalion was issued with two machine guns. Officers on the newly-reformed General Staff had great faith in the regular soldiers, but did not much trust the Territorials — 'a part-time Army'. And it was the small, professional Army which was sent to France in August 1914 when Germany annexed Belgium and forced the Liberal government to declare war.

47 The huge lion in the Forbury Gardens, Reading, a memorial to the men of the Berkshire Regiment who fell at the Battle of Maiwand, 27 July 1880 — one of the many dramatic defeats suffered by the British in Afghanistan.

9. The First World War, 1914-18

The Old Contemptibles

In August 1914 Sir John French led six infantry divisions and one cavalry division into battle against Germany. On 24 September 1914 Army Headquarters issued a statement:

> The following is a copy of Orders issued by the German Emperor on 19 August: *'It is my Royal and Imperial command that you should concentrate your energies for the immediate present upon one single person, that is that you address all your skill and all the valour of my soldiers to exterminate first, the treacherous English, walk over General French's contemptible little army.'* Headquarters, Aix-la-Chapelle, 19 August.

48 Volunteers for the 5th Battalion of the Dorsetshire Regiment being instructed in the position of 'Attention' at the Depot, Dorchester, in August 1914.

49 A recruiting poster issued in 1915 to encourage men to volunteer for the Army. In spite of such propaganda the government was forced to bring in a Conscription Act to ensure that enough men were available.

The results of this order were the operations commencing with Mons, and the advance of the seemingly overwhelming masses against us. The answer of the British Army on the subject of extermination has already been given.

Printing Co, R E 69

This is the origin of the term 'the old contemptibles' which Britain's professional Army proudly took for its title. It seems, however, that the German Kaiser had never issued any such order. He himself wrote: 'On the contrary, I continually emphasized the high value of the British Army, and often, indeed, in peacetime gave warning against underestimating it.'

The statement issued on 24 September was just a piece of propaganda put out by the leaders of the British Army who hoped to rouse their men to anger; they certainly succeeded.

50 Allied troops landing in Anzac Bay during the Gallipoli campaign, 1915. Severe casualties resulted both from the battle and from the insanitary conditions.

It is difficult, if not impossible, for us today to understand the enthusiasm with which the British entered into war in 1914. A young poet, Rupert Brooke, wrote: 'Now God be thanked who had matched us with this Hour.' The war against Germany was seen as some kind of holy war in which the virtuous British were going to oppose the wicked 'Hun', as the Germans were nicknamed. The professionals went to France, some hoping that 'it would all be over by Christmas'; others agreed with Kitchener (now Secretary of State for War). He thought that the struggle would be hard and would last at least three years. He hoped that his professional Army would do well enough to allow him time to train a new Army from among the thousands of volunteers who flocked to the recruiting offices.

By the time the war had ended in November 1918, the British Army had fought in various parts of Africa, in Mesopotamia, Palestine, Gallipoli, the Balkans and Italy — and, of course, along the hundreds of miles of the Western Front in France. It will not be possible to write about many of the battles in which the men of the Army showed their heroic courage. I have picked out two — mainly because the outcome of these battles was particularly important.

The Marne, 1914

The Germans hoped to knock out France in a very quick campaign. To do this they followed a plan which had been drawn up by a German general, Schlieffen, in 1905. Schlieffen proposed that seven German armies should drive their way through Belgium and Northern France and, with a 'right hook', surround Paris. They would then continue until they came out behind the French armies on the Western Front. The French armies would be caught like a nut in a pair of crackers, and, said Schlieffen, would crumble. This entire movement was scheduled to take only 40 days.

At Mons the British Army came into head-on collision with the German armies driving through Belgium. About 100,000 British soldiers had their first taste of battle at Mons, by its canals and slag heaps. Here the Germans encountered the rapid British rifle fire — which had once defeated Napoleon's armies, and which, in 1914, was so fast and accurate that the Germans thought the British must have thousands of machine guns. As one German wrote: 'Well entrenched and completely hidden, the enemy opened a murderous fire . . . the casualties increased . . . the rushes became shorter and finally the whole advance stopped with bloody losses.'

But the British paid a high price; the Cheshire Regiment, for example, went into Mons with 27 officers and 1,007 men; when it ended only six officers and 129 men were alive. A British commander wrote:

> It was due to the gallant action of these two battalions [the other was the First Battalion the Royal Norfolk Regiment] that the division was able to extricate itself. The fact that this very heavy enemy attack was held long enough to allow the withdrawal of the division is sufficient testimony to the gallantry and devotion of the two battalions concerned.

The British Army was forced to retreat from Mons until, in October-November 1914, it made another stand against the Germans, at Ypres. Here again the Army faced a much larger force which was much better equipped. And yet, under the command of Sir Douglas Haig, the Army's discipline, rifle and fighting power held the Germans at bay. The historian Liddell Hart called Ypres: 'The supreme memorial to the British Regular Army.'

One corporal who fought at Ypres said: 'I saw a soldier, his belly ripped open, supporting his back against the trench while he gazed with fascinated eyes at large coils of his own guts, which he held in both hands.'

But the Germans had been delayed and their 40-day timetable had been thrown out of gear. Some of their commanders disobeyed orders, hoping to make up for time lost — and managed to reach the River Marne only a few miles from Paris. But their line was no longer as orderly as it was supposed to be according to the Schlieffen Plan, and the French Marshal Joffre, together with Sir John French, led the French and British armies into the final stages of the Battle of the Marne. The Germans were driven back until they had crossed the River Aisne, where they dug themselves in. Winston Churchill wrote:

One must suppose that the Marne was the greatest battle ever fought in the world... but it was like no other battle. Comparatively few were killed or wounded, and no great recognizable feat of arms, and no shock proportionate to the event can be discerned.

This battle was important because it was the last time in which there was any great movement of men and materials; after the Marne both sides settled down to the long drawn-out and completely new trench warfare. The Battle of the Marne is also important because it involved the British in the sacrifice of their regular Army. This gave even greater urgency to Kitchener's campaign for volunteers, and the influx of these new men changed the face of the British Army. From then on it became very much a people's Army as it had never been before.

The Somme, 1916

By July 1916 the warring enemies seemed to have reached a stalemate; each had dug trenches that reached from the Alps to the Belgian coast; each tried to shift the other — with artillery bombardment, small raids on enemy trenches,

51 Trench warfare. One soldier looks over the top, one sleeps under the shelter of a cape, and another is dead. Notice the loose earth which was quickly turned into mud when the rains came. Notice also the litter and the makeshift wooden steps.

52 Even in the trenches, the British Tommy was supposed to carry around a mass of equipment, to wear puttees and to be prepared to appear in parade-drill uniform.

mortar and rifle attacks. But there was none of that movement which had characterized past campaigns — when Marlborough, Wellington, Roberts and other leaders had marched their men over long distances to meet and defeat an enemy. Trench warfare was unlike anything that the Army had known; one soldier wrote:

> The trench is empty... corpses lie along the parados, rotting in the wet; every now and then a booted foot appears jutting over the trench. The mud makes it all but impassable, and now, sunk in it up to the knees, I have the momentary terror of never being able to pull myself out... This is the very limit of endurance!

Some men were unable to face such a seemingly endless and meaningless existence. Brigadier Crozier wrote:

> I saw a strong rabble of tired, hungry and thirsty stragglers approach from the east. I go out to meet them, 'Where are you going?' I ask. One says one

thing, one another. They are marched to the water reserve, given a drink and hunted back to fight. Another more formidable party cuts across to the south. They mean business. They are damned if they are going to stay, it's all up. A young sprinting subaltern heads them off. They push by him. He draws his revolver and threatens them. They take no notice. He fires. Down drops a British soldier at his feet. The effect is instantaneous. They turn back to the assistance of their comrades in distress.

In the summer of 1916 Sir Douglas Haig decided to make a great effort to break the stalemate, drive the Germans from their positions, advance past their positions and so win the war by one great battle. The German trenches were defended by belts of barbed wire about 20-30 yards (18-26 metres) wide. This barbed wire would make an infantry advance impossible so it had to be cut. At 7.00 am on 23 June, the British artillery opened fire and for a whole week about 300 guns poured shells solidly onto the German positions. One artillery lieutenant wrote:

It seemed to throb in our veins, and then, at last, ten minutes before zero, the guns opened their lungs. For a mile, stretching away from me, the trench was belching forth dense columns of white, greenish and orange smoke. It rose, curling and testing, blotting everything from view. It seemed impossible that men could withstand this awful onslaught.

Another soldier wrote: 'The air seemed to be full of a vast and agonized violence, bursting now into groans and sighs, now into shrill screaming and pitiful whimperings, shuddering beneath terrible blows, torn by unearthly whips!'

On 30 June Haig entered in his diary: 'Preparations were never so thorough, nor troops better trained. Wire very well cut and ammunition adequate.'

But Haig was wrong; a good deal of the wire was untouched, and where gaps had appeared the Germans had simply rolled new wire in. Haig's ignorance of front-line conditions was due in part to the size of the Army and to the complexity of administering a front line which stretched for hundreds of miles. Previous commanders such as Marlborough and Wellington had been with their men, known to them, participating in the battle at first hand. But in this war the commander was unable to be everywhere at once — and so thought it best to remain behind the battalion lines in order to receive reports from all sectors, and keep an eye on the whole front, via maps, runners' reports and telephone communication. This helps to explain the entry in Haig's diary for 1 July 1916: 'Hard fighting continued all day on front of Fourth Army. On a 16-mile front of attack varying fortunes must be expected.'

On that first of July the bombardment had stopped, and at dawn men were ordered to fix bayonets. Whistles blew as a signal to attack and 100,000 men scrambled out of their trenches. As one wrote: 'No fuss, no shouting, no running, everything solid and thorough — just like the men themselves. All had a cheery face.'

A German who saw the advance wrote of it:

They came on at a steady easy pace as if expecting to find nothing alive in our trenches... Whole sections seemed to fall, and the rear formations, moving in close order, quickly scattered. The advance rapidly crumbled under this hail of shells and bullets. All along the line men could be seen throwing up their arms and collapsing, never to move again.

The men died because there were no gaps in the wire through which they could advance — or at least so few gaps that the men bunched together, making easy targets for the German machine gunners. On that first day, 60,000 out of the 100,000 men lost their lives. Many were killed outright; as Crozier wrote: 'I saw a wall of corpses.' Many others were wounded and drowned in the mud created by the terrific bombardment of the previous weeks. By 18 July another 20,000 men had been lost. By the time Haig called off the offensive, the British Army had suffered 400,000 casualties. Haig may have been satisfied with the attack but the new poets had none of Rupert Brooke's 'God be thanked' attitude. Siegfried Sassoon wrote:

> 'Good morning; good-morning!' the General said
> When we met him last week on our way to the line.
> Now the soldiers he smiled at are most of 'em dead,

53 Stretcher bearers carry away a wounded man during the Third Battle of Ypres, 1 August 1917.

54 British tanks in action during the Battle of the Somme, 1916. This was the first time that tanks had ever been used in battle.

And we're cursing his staff for incompetent swine.
'He's a cheery old card,' grunted Harry to Jack
As they slogged up to Arras with rifle and pack.
But he did for them both by his plan of attack.

There was one chance that the British might have broken through the German lines — by using a new weapon that had been devised. This was a tank about 7ft (2m) high and 32ft (9m) long, which could travel at about 3 mph. Fifty of these tanks had been built, but only 32 of them ever reached the battlefield. Of these only 24 were fit to go into battle — the others had broken down or were waiting for spare parts. Most of the 24 got bogged down in the mud, or were knocked out by artillery fire. Only four managed to achieve any damage — when they drove the enemy out of the village of Fleurs. But even that advantage was not followed up, and by evening these four had also been captured or destroyed.

The British losses at the Somme were severe — Winston Churchill has described the battle as 'the graveyard of Kitchener's Army' of volunteers. German losses at 600,000 and French losses at 200,000 were equally appalling.

The main contenders in the First World War were bled white at the Battle of the Somme, which came to an end when heavy snow fell on 17 and 18 November, making any further movement impossible.

Peace-Time Soldiering, 1919-39

In November 1918 the 'Great War' as it was called came to an end, and the British Army resumed its role as defender of the frontiers of the Empire — which did not become a Commonwealth until 1932. The Army also resumed its character as a professional Army, since conscription ended at the end of the war. But the Army of the 1920s and 1930s was very different from the pre-war Army. There were new weapons — such as the tank — which demanded a new kind of soldier. New regiments were formed, including the Royal Armoured Corps, the Royal Corps of Electrical and Mechanical Engineers, and others. Infantrymen who had to use Bren guns, mortars and anti-tank weapons had to acquire new skills.

All this meant that the British Army of the 1920s and 1930s needed a different type of recruit — more educated than his predecessors had been, more adaptable, and capable of much more initiative. To help these men achieve their best, the Army had to devise new systems of training. The old-fashioned 'square-bashing' fell very low down the scale, and battle drill became both more important and more realistic.

During the years 1920-39, British industry suffered from a series of economic depressions and there was a high level of unemployment. This helps to explain the high quality of recruit which the Army attracted in these inter-war years. 'Jack Frost' (or economic hardship) was still the best recruit. And the recruits had to be active — they fought wars in Afghanistan, they helped to put down an Arab revolt in Iraq, and to maintain law and order in Palestine. They served as garrison troops in Hong Kong and throughout India, as well as in various parts of colonial Africa, Malaya, Burma and the West Indies. Very rightly the recruiting poster declared: 'Join the Army and see the world!'

55 British troops wearing gas masks. Notice the primitive wireless-telegraph with which local commanders tried to keep in touch with events at the front.

10. The Second World War, 1939-45

In August 1939, Lord Beaverbrook's *Daily Express* assured its readers that there was not going to be war 'this year' — yet within days of this headline Britain was at war with Germany again. Very few thoughtful people agreed, however, with Beaverbrook's optimistic view of the future. Indeed, as early as 1938, the Chamberlain government, which had done so much to ensure that war could not break out, had itself passed the Act which brought back conscription, so that every man between the ages of 18 and 41 was liable for military service.

When the war did break out there was none of the fervour or hysteria that had been a feature of 1914; no poet expressed the views of Rupert Brooke (see page 74). One reason for this was the still-vivid memory of the bloodbath of the First World War; not even the most fervent patriot could wish to see a renewal of carnage on that scale.

The New Soldiers

The small professional Army welcomed a large number of recruits in 1938, and continued to conscript men right through the war. The new recruits were quite different from those who had volunteered in 1914 — they were better fed and better educated, medically fitter and much less subservient. They were also, as General Wavell observed, 'much softer and needed toughening' — a result of the rise of living standards that was a feature of British life in the inter-war years.

Soldiers in the Second World War were, in general, better led than their predecessors. There was a great deal of comradeship between junior officers and their men; officers seemed to be more relaxed than the officers had been in 1914; there was a great deal more 'mucking in', particularly in more remote theatres of war such as Burma and North Africa. Senior officers were also generally better trained, more understanding of the men's problems, and anxious to 'put them in the picture'. Officers now accepted that the better-educated soldiers deserved to be kept informed, and believed that informed men would be better equipped to fight well. At the highest level the Army was fortunate that it had leaders of the calibre of Field Marshals Slim (in Burma), Montgomery (in Africa and later in Europe), Alexander (in Africa and later in Italy). Even though they controlled thousands of men and tons of equipment, and their commands covered many square miles of territory, these commanders somehow managed to appear to be in touch with their men – as Marlborough and Wellington had been, and as Haig had not. Montgomery himself wrote: 'I issued orders that in the event of enemy attack, there would be *no* withdrawal. We would fight on the ground we now held, and if we couldn't stay there alive, we would stay there dead.' This stubbornness of their leader appealed to the men under Montgomery's command in North Africa.

The soldier who fought between 1939 and 1945 was not as tough, but was more educated and less subservient than his predecessors had been. His education was put to good use in the many battles of the Second World War, for it was a war of movement, of swift attacks. Commanders might have laid down an overall plan and junior commanders might have given detailed instructions to the men in their battalions. But once the battle had started, the individual soldier was thrown onto his own resources in a way which Wellington and even Haig would have found incredible. No more were the men to be chess pieces to be moved at the will of their commander. They were now free-willed pieces, moving under their own volition and not under orders, reacting to moves made by the enemy, and isolated in their tanks or armoured cars.

The various skills of the better-educated soldiers were put to good use in an Army which was increasingly dependent on technical ability. Men were trained as electricians and mechanics, engineers, wireless operators, intelligence personnel. There were still the many who walked with rifle and bayonet — but for every soldier who fought in this way, there were seven others who supplied, maintained and equipped him. Among these seven were the variously skilled men.

But the softer, better-educated soldier also showed during this war that he had the courage and tenacity of his forebears. Sir John Moore's greatest feat

56 'The Withdrawal from Dunkirk', a painting by Charles Cundall.

was, perhaps, the safe withdrawal of his men from Portugal; his grave at Corunna is a fitting memorial to a great general. In the Second World War there was an even greater withdrawal — from Dunkirk. On 10 May 1940 the Germans attacked the British and French armies along a wide front stretching from Belgium to Luxembourg. The Allies outnumbered the Germans but the latter were better equipped — with tanks, artillery and supporting aircraft. By 23 May 1940, 240,000 British and 80,000 French soldiers were cut off in the Dunkirk area with their backs to the sea. Then Hitler issued an order which stopped his victorious army from launching a final knock-out blow against the besieged enemy. General Guderian, a German tank commander, wrote: 'We were stopped within sight of Dunkirk. We watched the Luftwaffe attack. We also saw the armada of great and little ships by means of which the British were evacuating their forces.'

The German Air Force launched its attacks. One British officer described how 'the streets were blocked with rubble'. And yet this mass of men was withdrawn in spite of the German air attack, and under the very eyes of the German army. One reason for this successful withdrawal was the willingness of the Royal Navy and the owners of an armada of small boats to risk their lives in approaching the beach, from which they lifted the men. But a major reason for

57 British armoured troops in the North African desert.

its success was the quiet, calm discipline of the 'soft' soldier. As one officer wrote:

> Everyone had a blind faith in the Navy ... we tacked ourselves on to the rear of the smallest of three queues, the head of it was already standing in water up to the waist. Suddenly a small rowing boat appeared. The head of the queue got in and we moved up into the blackness ... our only thoughts were to get on a boat ... not a word was spoken ... heads and shoulders only above water ... praying that a boat would appear. It was like a slaughter-house on a hot day, the boats came in and took incredible risks, many were hit but the men still filed on, making piers out of piles of bren gun carriers, spanning shell holes with planks, and overall the smoke and noise grew thicker.

El Alamein

People rejoiced at the 'miracle of Dunkirk' although they agreed with Prime Minister Churchill: 'We must be very careful not to assign to this delivery the attributes of a victory. Wars are not won by evacuations.'

El Alamein was the first conclusive victory won by the British and marked a

58 Montgomery (without a hat) seen with members of his staff in North Africa.

59 Troops dug in before El Alamein.

major turning point in the history of the war. After Alamein, it seemed there were no defeats. On 13 August 1942 General Montgomery arrived to take charge of the British forces in North Africa. He found a depressed Army which had just lost Tobruk to Rommel's tank divisions; it seemed that the way to Cairo, the Suez Canal, the oilfields of the Middle East and maybe even India, was wide open to the Germans.

The confident leadership provided by Montgomery is reflected in his writing: 'I understood Rommel was expected to attack *us* shortly. If he came soon it would be tricky, if he came in a week all right, but give us two weeks and Rommel could do what he liked; he would be seen off and then it would be our turn.'

Rommel did attack — and was surprised by the preparations that Montgomery had made. Montgomery wrote:

> I was expecting such an attack. I would not allow our tanks to rush out at him; we would stand firm in the Alamein position, hold the Ruweisat and Alam Halfa Ridges securely, and let him beat up against them. We would fight a static battle and my forces would not move; his tanks would come up against our tanks dug-in hull down positions at the western edge of the Alam Halfa Ridge.

And then, on 23 October, Montgomery moved to the attack. Captain Murray of the Seaforths wrote:

Suddenly the whole horizon went pink and for a second or two there was still perfect silence, and then the noise of the 8th Army's guns hit us in a solid wall of sound that made the whole earth shake. Through the din we made out other sounds — the whine of shells overhead, the chatter of the machine guns and eventually the pipes. Then we saw a sight that will live for ever in our memories — line upon line of steel-helmeted figures with rifles at high port, bayonets catching in the moonlight, and over all the wailing of the pipes.

The greatest tank battle that the world had ever known started then and lasted until 4 November, when divisions of Highland and Indian troops broke through the German lines, and Rommel retreated rather than have his forces surrounded. The 'soft' soldier had shown his courage as well as his initiative.

Some Aspects of the War
The British Army fought in many and varied theatres of war. One soldier described a day in the North African war:

It was an ordinary Libyan day, furnace-hot, with a glare that was like a knife across the eyes. The sky was the colour of smoke. The sun was seen through it like a coin in a dim pool. Sixth platoon sat in their pits. Their shorts were bleached to a dirty yellow and their boots to whiteness by the sand. Those who had discarded their shirts showed skins as brown as the wood in the butts of their rifles. These were the men who were proud to call themselves the Desert Rats.

Slim's 'Forgotten Army' fought to prevent the Japanese following up their successes with the capture of India. In Italy, British troops played a large part in the successful drive up the peninsula. In Europe, under Eisenhower's overall command, Montgomery's troops took part in the invasion and the sweep through France and North Germany.

It is right to talk about a sweep — because this was a war of movement in which tanks and armoured cars, lorries and aircraft were used as never before. This involved a great deal of cooperation between various allies — American,

60 Back again. Troops landing in Normandy on D Day, 6 June 1944.

French, Polish, Canadian, British — and between the various arms of the Services. The Royal Navy played a large part, not only in the withdrawal from Dunkirk but also in the later invasions of France and Italy; the Royal Air Force acted as a shield for the naval forces during those invasions, and was then a valuable supporting arm for the ground troops in their march through Europe.

Wellington and Marlborough had had to concern themselves about feeding their troops. Commanders in the Second World War also had to do this; but in addition they had to consider the very great problem of maintaining and servicing hundreds of tanks, thousands of lorries and armoured vehicles. One armoured division would use up to 70,000 gallons (320,000 litres) of fuel a day — and this fuel had to be available if the forward progress was to be maintained.

Airborne Troops
In 1932 the first battalion of the Northamptonshire Regiment was airlifted from Ismailia to Baghdad. This was the first time that a complete unit had been flown into action. The British Army was slow to follow up this initiative, and even slower to follow the German example by forming special airborne troops. However, in time, the British learned the lesson. In June 1944, airborne troops took part in the invasion of Europe. Chester Wilmot, a BBC war correspondent, travelled with the first of them:

> The soil of France rushes past, and we touch with a jolt on a ploughed field. The glider careers on with grinding brakes and creaking timbers, snapping off five stout poles in its path. There is an ominous sound of splitting wood and rending fabric, and the glider goes lurching and bumping until it finally comes to rest scarred but intact within a hundred yards of its intended landing place. It is 3.32 am. We are two minutes late. Shouts and cheers echo down the glider, and a voice from the dark interior cries out: 'This is it, chum, I told yer we wouldn't 'av ter swim!'

Montgomery used an Airborne Division at Arnhem when he tried to capture the bridge over the lower Rhine in an attempt to compel the more cautious Eisenhower to drive the Allied Army forward to capture the important German industrial complex of the Ruhr. The courage of these troops caused one German commentator to note: 'The British Army fought like lions,' while a

61 Men of the 6th Airborne Division prepare to take off for an attack on a German base.

62 British troops search for Germans in a wrecked Dutch school. These troops had to use their own initiative as they went about their work.

Dutch housewife noted: 'You are an ordinary soldier, but your culture is that of all the British, of all the Airborne Division. With death or imprisonment before your eyes you have found that marvellously pure comradeship and simple strength of mind.'

Subservient to the USA

Marlborough had dominated Europe in his time; Wellington had been 'the Great Duke' in his time. But in 1944 and 1945, the British Army and its leaders only formed part, and, relatively speaking, a small part of the Allied armies that swept through Europe, freed Italy, France, Belgium, Holland, and finally reached Berlin. The Allied armies were commanded by an American, Eisenhower; American factories poured out much of the material and equipment which the Allied forces were using. Montgomery and Alexander were minor players on a stage where Americans walked tall.

The history of the British Army is, as we have seen, a reflection of the history of the British people. When Britain was one of the world's leading powers — if not the greatest — its Army and that Army's commanders were important figures. When the British lost their dominant position in the world — to be replaced by the Russians on the one hand and the Americans on the other — the British Army too became less important than it had been. But we would do well to remember what Eric Linklater wrote in 1953:

> Everything we have and are is ours, and still exists, by grace and courage of the soldiers. They are the men of the century, because without them we should no longer be numbering in years — or numbering them only to curse the wretchedness of our survival in it.

11. A Post-War Postscript, 1945-70

A Professional Army Again
By June 1945 the British Army numbered about 2,920,000 men, most of them conscripted under the terms of the 1938 Conscription Act. Once the Second World War had ended with the defeat of Germany and of Japan, the government set about releasing these war-hardened conscripts and, by 1949, they had all returned to civilian life. However, for a time, the government continued to conscript young men on their eighteenth birthday, mainly because the international situation remained gloomy, with the threat of a Third World War breaking out over Berlin in 1948, and over Korea in 1950.

However, in the 1950s the danger of war receded as a 'thaw' replaced the 'cold war', and in 1960 the British government brought conscription to an end. Since then the Army has been a volunteer, professional force of about 165,000 men, including about 19,000 officers.

No Longer a Great Power
As we have seen, the history of the British Army reflects the history of the British people, and this is as true of post-war Britain as it was of the Britain of Marlborough or Wellington. Modern Britain is unable to match the giant powers – Russia, the USA, China – in their military competence. Only these great powers can afford the latest weapons – missiles with nuclear warheads, submarines driven by nuclear power and carrying nuclear missiles, gigantic rockets which can fly many thousands of miles, and, we are told, land with pinpoint accuracy on their targets. Britain is no longer one of the great powers, and she has been obliged to make a number of military agreements with friends and allies by which Britain puts some of her forces at the disposal of the commander of the allied forces. The North Atlantic Treaty Organization (NATO) is one such military agreement by which about 50,000 British troops are left in Germany (forming the British Army on the Rhine), and form part of the NATO force which exists to counter the threat of a Russian invasion of Western Europe.

The USA Leads the West
Long ago British politicians and Army commanders used to speak for 'our' side in any struggle. Politicians such as Palmerston, Lloyd George and Winston Churchill played a leading role on the world's stage; military commanders such as Wellington, Marlborough and Haig were accepted as allied leaders in wartime. Since 1945 Britain has had to give up her former position of world leader; she has been replaced by the USA as 'champion of the West'.

Britain's Army reflects this supporting role. In 1948 it seemed that the Russians were trying to take over Berlin; it was the US Air Force which provided the bulk of the aid to the besieged Berliners, to whom everything had to be flown in. British soldiers played their part — loading and unloading the aircraft. In 1949 the Communists of North Korea, aided by the Russians and later by the Chinese, attacked the American-supported government of South Korea. It was an American army which formed the bulk of the United Nations Army which was sent to Korea to drive the Communists back. Throughout the three years of the Korean War, small British detachments fought alongside and under the command of their more powerful American allies.

The Sun Sets over the Empire

Since 1945 the British have, maybe reluctantly, withdrawn from their former colonies. Independence has been granted to the people of India, Ceylon,

63 British troops helping to feed refugees in Central Europe at the end of the Second World War. One of the continuing features of the history of the British Army has been the kindness of its officers and men when the fighting is over. 'We are not', said Wellington, 'a military nation.'

64 The Army in action in Belfast, August 1971. Notice the walkie-talkie being used by one soldier. Notice also that these men are no longer 'pieces' being 'moved' by a nearby commander. They have to use their own initiative to deal with the situation.

Ghana, Nigeria, Uganda, Cyprus, Malta, Aden and so on. Sometimes the handover was a peaceful affair; the Army's contribution to the independence of countries such as India was a matter of ceremonial — garrisons were withdrawn, flags lowered for the last time, regimental airs played on docksides and the troops brought home.

Sometimes, however, there was a more bloody prelude to independence; the Army was called on to fight against rebels in Aden, and terrorists in Kenya and Cyprus. In such guerilla wars the Army was hampered by the presence of a hostile population, who aided the rebels and the terrorists. They also faced the criticism of a British press which picked on the infrequent examples of brutality or misbehaviour and tended to ignore the day-to-day behaviour of the Army. It is worthwhile recalling that in 1964, when the governments of East Africa — former colonial territories — felt themselves threatened by a wave of terrorism and rebellion, it was the British Army they sent for to help them out. This was a good advertisement for the Army.

Garrisons and Police Duties

The British Army still maintains garrisons in those few parts of the world today which are not yet self-governing, such as Hong Kong. We also maintain a garrison in some self-governing territories, such as Gibraltar. But more newsworthy have been the activities of the Army acting as a kind of police force — in Guiana and, nearer home, in Northern Ireland. In such areas the Army has been called on, not so much to put down a rebellion or a terrorist uprising, but to keep apart two warring factions inside the host country. In the early 1970s, there were many TV programmes which dealt with the Army's role in Northern Ireland. I watched one such programme only recently and noted, again, how the Army is a mirror of our society. In the ranks of the British Army in Northern Ireland there are a number of coloured immigrant recruits — men who were perhaps born overseas and have come to live in Britain, or who were born in Britain to immigrant parents. The presence of these men in the small professional Army is a reminder of the growth in the number of coloured immigrants in the 1950s and 1960s. It was also noticeable that there was a very relaxed, almost companionable, relationship between officers and men; there was none of the old-fashioned 'us and them' attitude — and this again is a reflection of what has happened in Britain as a whole in the last 30 years. I was impressed by the large degree of initiative which the ordinary soldier was expected to use as he patrolled the Belfast streets, searching suspects, confronting a dangerous-looking crowd, on the look-out for gunmen. There was none of the 'chess pieces' mentality of the Wellington Army.

But the main impression left by the programme was that the modern recruit is a man who is well-behaved, well-spoken and orderly, like the rest of the British people. Wellington had called his men 'the scum of the earth', and Kipling had commented on ordinary people's reluctance to allow soldiers near their homes, public houses or theatres. But the modern soldier at work in Belfast allowed the various factions there to stone him, spit and jeer — and in private admitted 'I feel sorry for them'.

A Smaller Army
The modern Army contains a more educated type of soldier, who is expected to use his own initiative. He also uses a great deal of modern equipment — from the walkie-talkie which is clipped to his uniform up to the huge tanks with their sophisticated weapons. The days of the infantryman are not altogether numbered, but far fewer are needed than in the days when columns of infantry marched into battle. One sign of this change has been the 'death' of many famous regiments. Each infantry regiment has been reduced from two battalions to one, and a number of the smaller regiments have been amalgamated. There was a good deal of opposition to such a massive change, and stickers, such as 'Save the Argylls', sprouted on car windows.

However, the amalgamation went on, in the Army as it did in civil life — where fewer but larger firms now control banking, brewing, building, aircraft building and so on. The Army is indeed still reflecting what is happening in society as a whole.

65 Chelsea Pensioners being shown over the new Chelsea Barracks, July 1962. These veterans must envy the life enjoyed by the young soldiers who are showing them around their new home. The soldiers of today are better paid, clothed, armed, commanded, educated and housed than ever the old soldiers used to be.

Further Information

Documentary material
I wish to acknowledge my debt to:
Laffin, John, *Tommy Atkins* (Cassell).
Ward, Marjorie, *The Blessed Trade* (Michael Joseph).
These two books contain many excellent first-hand accounts of life in the Army.

There are also:
Briggs, Asa, *They Lived Like This, 1700-1815* (Blackwell).
Briggs, Asa, *They Lived Like This, 1897-1940* (Blackwell).
Edwards, Charles, *They Saw it Happen, 1689-1897* (Blackwell).

Then and There Series, published by Longman:
Clarke, G, *The American Revolution*.
Murphy, E, *Cavaliers and Roundheads*.
Speed, P F, *Wellington's Army*.
Sylvester, D W, *Clive in India*.

Sentinel Series, published by Wayland:
Gibson, Michael, *Cavaliers and Roundheads*.
Holden, Matthew, *The Desert Rats*.
Holden, Matthew, *War in the Trenches*.
Jeffreys, Steven, *A Medieval Siege*.

Films
16 mm filmstrips, produced by Rank:
The Civil War in England.
The Anglo-French Struggle in North America.
The American Revolution.
The Second World War.

Places to Visit
The headquarters of your nearest regiment (consult Taylor, *Discovering English County Regiments,* Shire Publications).
The Imperial War Museum.
The National Army Museum.
Your nearest Army Information Centre.

INDEX

The numbers in **bold** indicate pages on which illustrations appear.

Afghanistan, 54, 55, 67, 81; **54, 71**
Africa, 57, 66, 74, 81-87; **84, 85**
airborne troops, 88, 89; **88**
Alexander, Field Marshal, 82, 89
Alfred, King, 9
Anglo-Saxons, 9
archers, 13, 14; **11**
armour, 14-17, 20; **15, 16**
artillery, 14, 17, 21, 51, 76, 78, 80, 84; **20, 53**

barracks, 26, 43, 44, 63, 70
Battles, Albuhera, 52, 60; **49**
 Arnhem, 88, 89
 Badajoz, 49; **50**
 Blenheim, 31-34; **30, 33, 34**
 Crécy, 14
 Dettingen, 39
 El Alamein, 85-87; **86**
 Hastings, 9, 10
 Inkerman, **60**
 Jellalabad, 55; **54**
 Mafeking, **65**
 Maiwand, **71**
 Marne, 75, 76
 Minden, 41; **40**
 Mons, 73, 75
 Poitiers, 14
 Somme, 76, 80, 81; **80**
 Waterloo, 45, 47, 48, 51; **52**
 Ypres, 75; **79**
Belgium, 75, 84, 89
billets, 25-27, 35
Boers, 65-70; **8, 65, 69, 70**
booty, 14, 17, 18, 29, 31, **50**
Braddock, General, 41
breeches, 34, 36, 46; **46**
bren guns, 81, 85

Canada, 6, 27, 28, 70; **41**
cannon, 17, 32, 39, 53; **20**
Cardwell, Edward, 62, 63, 70
castles, 11-14, 17; **11, 12**
cavalry, 5, 9, 11, 14, 18, 20, 21, 32, 38-42, 49, 51, 71, 72; **40**
Chamberlain, Joseph, 67, 69
 Neville, 82
Charles I, 20-23; **22**
Charles II, 6, 22, 28; **25**
Chelsea Hospital, 35, 43; **26, 52, 92**
China, 90, 91
Churchill, John, 26, 28
Churchill, Winston, 68, 69, 75, 80, 85, 90
Civil War, 6, 18, 20-23; **22, 23**
Commanders, 9, 13, 31, 33, 36, 38-42, 67, 68, 75, 78, 82, 83, 88, 90; **23, 30, 40, 41, 47, 81, 92**
commissions, 38, 45, 55, 62, 63
conscription, 81, 82, 90; **73**
Crimea, 58, 61, 62, 64; **7, 58, 61**
Cromwell, Oliver, 20, 21
crossbow, 13, 14; **11**
Crusaders, the, 12, 14

discipline, 12, 13, 20, 21, 27, 31, 44, 56, 71, 75, 81
disease, 15, 45, 47, 53, 57, 58, 70; **74**
drill, 31, 81
Dunkirk, 83-85, 88; **83**

Eisenhower, General, 87, 89
Empire, the British, 6, 28, 36-44, 53, 57, 63, 67, 70, 81, 91
Europe, 6, 27, 28, 39, 82, 87-89
executions, 56, 57

Fairfax, 18; **19**
feudal army, 10, 11
Flanders, 5, 8, 27, 34, 45, 76, 80, 81; **5**
flogging, 43, 46, 62
food, 25, 30, 34, 35, 42, 43, 46, 47, 49, 53, 56, 58, 60, 64
footmen, 9, 11, 27
fyrd, the 9, 17, 18

gaiters, 36, 41, 42, 47; **37**
Gallipoli, 74; **74**
George II, 36, 39
George III, 28
Germany, 28, 70, 71, 72-81, 82-89, 90
Gladstone, W E, 67, 68
grenadiers, 23, 24, 27, 51; **37**
Guards, the, 5, 22, 31, 40, 42, 51

Haig, General, 75, 78, 79, 82, 83, 90
hairstyles, 36, 46; **37, 46**
Haldane, R E, 70, 71
Harold, King, 9, 17
Henry I, 11
Henry VII, 17
Henry VIII, 17
horses, 5, 9, 10, 11, 14, 18, 20, 21, 30, 32, 38-42, 47, 49, 51, 58, 71, 72; **15, 40**
hospitals, 26, 53, 62, 64

95

India, 6, 8, 27, 28, 39, 48, 54-57, 68, 70, 81, 86, 87, 91, 92; **46, 56, 57**
infantrymen, 9, 11, 18, 20-24, 31, 38-42, 44, 49, 51, 71, 72, 81, 92; 37, **40, 47, 53, 77**
Ireland, 27; **16**
Italy, 74, 82, 87-89

James II, 26, 44
Japan, 8, 87, 90

Kabul, 54, 67
Khartoum, 67, 68
Kipling, Rudyard, 35, 66, 68, 92
Kitchener, Lord, 68, 70, 74, 80
knights, 9, 11, 13, 17; **11, 15**

Ladysmith, 69, 70
Light Brigade, 61, 62; **7, 61**
longbow, 14; **11**
looting, 14, 17, 18, 29, 31

machine guns, 71, 75, 79, 87
Mafeking, 70; **70**
Mahrattas, 6; **46**
marching, 29, 30, 39, 40, 47, 48, 55, 66, 77; **56**
Marlborough, Duke of, 28-36, 77, 78, 82, 88, 89, 90; **33, 34**
medical services, 35, 47, 48, 53, 57, 60, 62
mercenary soldiers, 9, 12, 17, 18
militia, 17, 71
Montgomery, Field Marshal, 82, 86-89; **85**
Moore, Sir John, 45, 46, 83
muskets, 17, 18, 20, 21, 42, 46, 62, 70; **16, 24, 40**

Napoleon, 6, 45, 51, 75
NATO, 90
Nightingale, Florence, 60, 61
Normans, the, 9-13; **11, 12**

officers, 20, 21, 45-49, 55, 58, 61, 62, 65, 68-71, 75, 78, 82, 92; **47, 48, 60, 69**

Parliament, 6, 12, 18, 20-22, 35; **19**
pay, 21, 25, 26, 27, 42, 43, 46, 47, 56, 62, 64, 70
pensions, 43, 62
pigtail, 36, 41
pikemen, 18-21; **16, 40**
Pitt, the Elder, 41, 42
Pitt, the Younger, 38, 43
plunder, 14, 29, 31, 50
Portugal, 9, 34, 45, 47, 84; **48**
punishments, 27, 42-44, 46, 56
purchase (of commissions), 38, 45, 55, 62, 63; **6**

recruits, 18, 19, 21-27, 33, 34, 41, 58, 62-66, 74, 76, 81, 82, 92; **63, 72, 73**
redcoats, 21, 34, 35, 68; **37, 46, 66**
regiments, 5, 7, 21-25, 28, 34-41, 43, 45, 54, 55, 62-64, 67, 75, 87, 88, 92; **37, 40, 63, 69, 71, 72**
Remembrance Day, 5, 8; **5**
Richard I, 12, 14
Roberts, Lord, 67, 68, 70, 77
Russia, 6, 58, 61-63, 70, 89-91

sieges, 13, 14, 17, 23, 28, 29, 35; **11, 13**
Slim, Field Marshal, 82, 87
Spain, 28, 34, 36, 38, 45; **38**

tanks, 80-84, 86-88, 92; **80, 84**
Territorial Army, 71
trenches, 76-78; **76**
Turkey, 12, 14 16

uniforms, 20, 21, 36-44; **65, 66, 77**
USA, the, 90, 91

Victoria Cross, 61

Wars, Afghan, 54, 55; **54, 71**
 Ashanti, 57
 Boer, 65-70; **8, 65, 66, 69**
 Burmese, 53; **54**
 Civil, 6, 18, 20-23; **22**
 Crimean, 58-64; **7, 59, 60, 61**
 Crusader, 12, 14
 First World, 5, 6, 72-81
 Jenkins Ear, 36, 38; **38**
 Korean, 90, 91
 of the Roses, 17
 Second World, 5, 6, 82-90
 Sikh, 55
 Zulu, 57
Wellington, Duke of, 9, 39, 45-52, 77, 78, 82, 83, 88-92; **6, 46, 47, 48, 50, 52, 91**
Western Front, 74, 75
West Indies, 28, 36, 81
William the Conqueror, 9, 10; **10**

York, Duke of, 22, 28, 45